201st Squadron:

The Aztec Eagles

The History of the Mexican Pilots
Who Fought in World War II

GUSTAVO VÁZQUEZ LOZANO

201st Squadron: The Aztec Eagles.
The History of the Mexican Pilots who Fought in World War II
Copyright © 2017 by Gustavo Vázquez Lozano

Translated by Amber Aguilar

First English edition: 2019
Revised and expanded
Published by Libros de México

www.librosdemexico.org
librosdemexico@gmail.com

ISBN: 978-0-9970858-8-4

"Under the burden of that black night of humanity, rekindled by current international events, they still live in my thoughts, full of life: the comrades with whom one fine day, sheltered by the symbols of Mexico, we sailed into the sun, to fight for peace and freedom."

Ricardo Blanco, member of the FAEM

TABLE OF CONTENTS

THE PILOTS AFTER THEIR FIRST COMBAT MISSION

MEXICAN PROPAGANDA, WWII

A HEROES' WELCOME, NOVEMBER 1945

A note about the photographs

The photographs of the 201st Squadron, on its training in the United States and the war in the Philippines, come from different sources. With contributions from relatives of the pilots, out of print books published in the 1940s, photocopies, newspapers of the era, and the internet, a small collection of images of different qualities was gathered. Many originals are lost because they were extracted from the national archives, and others are impossible to locate. The different qualities of the images in this book are due to this diversity of sources. Due to their historical and testimonial value, it seemed to me it was better to include them than to leave them out.

A special thanks to Dr. Mario Longoria of the University of Texas for facilitating access to his private collection, as well as to Sergeant Fernando Nava Musa, Sergeant Horacio Castilleja Albarrán, Second Lieutenant Juan López Murillo, Lieutenant Heriberto Cañete López, all of them members of the Expeditionary Force that went to the Philippines, as well as numerous relatives of FAEM members who contributed to this book with their memories.

The author

INTRODUCTION —Forgotten heroes

In April of 1945, just before the end of the Second World War, when it was clear who would triumph in Europe, Mexico sent an air contingent to fight shoulder-to-shoulder with the Allied Forces: its name was the 201st Fighter Squadron. The six-year war that had wrought so much havoc would be over in just three months: the group of Mexican pilots flew through the last, rapidly-closing gap in order to finish on the side of the victors. The Mexican Expeditionary Air Force (FAEM), the only Mexican armed detachment ever to fight overseas, comprised three hundred members from all over the country, from very young men to veterans of the Revolution. Its arrival in the Far East was a shot in the arm for the Allies on the brutal Pacific front.

The thirty pilots who made up the air squadron did not fight Nazi Germany or Italian fascism, but Japanese imperialism in Luzon and Formosa; their participation was brave and honorable, albeit modest and limited geographically to the Philippines and the South China Sea. The mission dripped with symbolism: during colonial times, the Philippines had been administrated from New Spain (modern-day Mexico), and there were —and still are— multiple cultural and social links between the two peoples. Mexicans had read of the atrocities of the Japanese occupation in the newspapers, and the battle to liberate the archipelago was a cause they could get behind. The best of the Mexican Air Force arrived in the Far East to form part of the end of the biggest naval battle in history, under the command of the legendary General Douglas MacArthur. To a large extent, it was the vision of the American ambassador to Mexico, George Messersmith, who recognized this historic opportunity, which made the involvement of the Mexican contingent possible; not forgetting

Mexico's president, Manuel Ávila Camacho, who offered backup to the United States as well as securing the moral support of the entire hemisphere. Ávila Camacho was the last soldier to serve as Mexican president, and as such, he knew about war. Although this has never been officially acknowledged, he saw the opportunity for his country to participate in the redistribution of territory following the Allies' victory, and a chance at a piece of the Philippines themselves. Who could have predicted what the state of international relations would be once the horror was over?

The great adventure of the 201st Squadron was a hastily-added footnote; a small Mexican coda on a worldwide conflagration that was already coming to an end. Back home, the exploits of the thirty pilots in charge of those Republic P-47 Thunderbolts had society in a state of excitement, and the faraway location lent any news of them a heroic, legendary air. Upon their return from the front, they were greeted triumphantly in Mexico City: streets were named after them and a colossal monument was erected in their honor in Chapultepec Forest, Mexico's place of heroes and martyrs.

But once the frenzy had passed, the young pilots were forgotten. In textbooks from their own country, they occupy at best a few lines and perhaps a tiny photograph. Many young people have never heard of them. Naturally, the Second World War would have ended the same way with or without their input. Their triumph lay not in the bombs they dropped on Luzon and Formosa, nor in the homages paid to them at home, nor in the kisses planted on them by young Filipina women, immortalized in iconic black-and-white photographs. Their greatest achievement was somewhat less ostentatious, but it was to prove more enduring: the 201st Squadron enabled Mexico to join the ranks of nations who lost sons on the battlefield, and leave the unaffected group of neutral countries. This changed things for Mexico.

The sacrifice of those who fought against the Japanese empire earned Mexico the respect of conquering powers and bought the country a one-way ticket to modernity, a voice in global post-war negotiations – specifically, a place among the forty-nine founders of the United Nations and the Security Council in 1946 – and, above all, an improvement to its hitherto hostile relationship with the US. For the first time in the two countries' history, they had joined forces against a common enemy. When those young Mexicans had entered the United States through Laredo in 1944, they had been looked down on and viewed with mistrust. On their return to Los Angeles in 1945, however, they were welcomed with open arms and floral displays. It would not be an exaggeration to state that it was at that moment that the modern diplomatic relationship between Mexico and the United States was born.

This new collaboration had innumerable benefits for Mexico; the end of the war heralded a long period of economic growth and peacetime for the country, which was to last nearly three decades. However, the movement towards the demilitarization of politics and government relegated the 201st Squadron to the status of mere anecdote. Mexican historians showed little interest in the Squadron: it became a subject more for television, radio and comic strips, often with historically inaccurate and unrealistic stories. Over in the States and other Allied countries, soldiers of the Second World War became the greatest generation; in Mexico they were soon all but forgotten. The election of the first civil president, Miguel Alemán, inaugurated the era of attorneys, the presidents graduated from law school, and, with a final flourish, it brought to a close the age of military men as presidents.

This is the history, told for the first time, of the 201st Squadron, and the thirty pilots –out of hundreds who volunteered– who won their place to fight in the skies and contribute, albeit modestly, to the fall of the Rome-Berlin-Tokyo Axis. Using unedited sources, declassified reports, old military files, and the testimonies of pilots and other contemporary witnesses, this new edition of the book revives important characters in order to detail the intricacies of the missions, heroic facts, and tragedies, and analyze the legacy of the 201st Squadron like never before.

I. DISTANT NEIGHBORS FIND A COMMON ENEMY

It was only thanks to the US that Mexico took part in the Second World War through the 201st Squadron, securing its place on the side of the victors. The most remarkable aspect of the matter is that the two countries had been historic enemies with few cordial periods (one of which was the presidency of Porfirio Díaz) and remained so until the late 1930s, when the great conflagration began. Tensions were rife between the two countries from 1823 to 1939, with armed interventions north to south, attempts at declaring war, diplomatic pressures, and massacres and acts of vengeance from both sides, albeit on different scales. In 1847, a war started by the US ended with the occupation of northern Mexico and the capital, and with the eventual hoisting of the US flag at the Palacio Nacional. For a few weeks, with the Mexican government in disarray, US General Winfield Scott acted as military governor of Mexico City.

After the war, and having taken for itself over half the territory of ancient Mexico, the titan of the north took every opportunity to reopen the debate regarding claims to the demarcation of the new border. Most noteworthy, almost to the point of sparking another invasion, was a dispute over the construction of the Pacific transcontinental railroad. The US had its sights set on a new frontier that not only involved the absorption of the small area named La Mesilla, through which the railway would pass; it also had designs on the peninsula of Baja

California and the states of Sonora, Sinaloa, Durango and Chihuahua. Mexico was informed that the US was prepared to go to war once again if the former refused to sell La Mesilla, and that the superpower would not hesitate to take away another half of that territory if this relatively minor matter was not resolved immediately.

The enduring peace of the Porfirio Díaz presidency was underpinned by generous concessions made by Díaz to American companies who understood that they no longer needed armies in order to extract whatever they needed from their neighbors to the south. Tensions were reignited during the Mexican Revolution, and threats of another intervention were hinted at, most explicitly in 1914 in the port city of Veracruz. In 1916, Francisco Villa pillaged the small town of Columbus in New Mexico. The American public were baying for his blood and sought retributions against those living south of the Rio Grande.

The Great Depression of the 1930s stoked animosity towards Mexicans in the States, and soaring unemployment was swiftly responded to with mass deportations. Almost two million people of Mexican origin were deported over the course of the decade, despite the fact that many of them had been born in the US. President Hoover promulgated laws prohibiting the employment of Mexicans by birth or ethnic background.

The nationalization of oil reserves and the expropriation of foreign industries by President Lázaro Cárdenas in 1938 sparked whispered rumors of a new war. The US was prepared to intervene once again in Mexico; Great Britain and other European nations joined them in expressing their intent to recover what they were owed. It seemed inevitable that the history of the military intervention of 1862 was to repeat itself; but with the onset of the Second World War, American and British diplomats began to realize that a threat greater than that posed by Mexico's nationalist policies was circling above their cities. The countries´ priorities had shifted. Miraculously, President Lázaro Cárdenas escaped reprisals.

The Second World War

In 1939, Mexico was a country devastated by four catastrophic decades: ten years of economic crisis (1900-1910) followed by civil war and rounded off by the global Great Depression. In the wake of the Mexican Revolution and the mass deportations of the 30s, hostility between Mexicans and Americans had reached boiling point. The majority of the population, from Chihuahua to Yucatán, knew nothing of the US beyond memories of invasions, disputes, exploitation, government privileges and the constant air of menace –always one-way. For this reason, when news came that the land of Washington, Jefferson and Lincoln had come under attack from a mightier power –the Rome-Berlin-Tokyo Axis– many Mexicans quietly celebrated. The Revolution at home had veered towards the left, and there was a strong undercurrent of sympathy with the Soviet Union. Mexico decided in the first instance to remain neutral in the Second World War and capitalize on the conflict by selling raw materials indiscriminately to Germany and to the States.

Also in 1935, Arthur Dietrich, who would play a fundamental role, was appointed Chief of the Press Office at the embassy in Mexico. His mission was to turn public opinion in favor of Nazism and against the Allies. From the embassy the money flowed to publishers □ pockets to finance a good number of publications, magazines and newspapers, which would be distributed massively among the population, especially the middle and upper classes. Dietrich subsidized existing newspapers, including those with the largest circulation, *Excélsior, El Universal* and *Novedades*, to print editorials, propaganda and news that were favorable to the Reich and put the Allies as imperialist monsters. Many opinion articles in El Universal and Excelsior described the United States as Mexico's greatest enemy. Nazi propagandists and their writers for hire extolled Germany's struggle against European imperialism and compared it to Mexico's resistance to the arrogant United States. They also exploited the fear of the middle class, especially businessmen, for communism.

However, disquiet was stirring in the country thanks to propaganda from German operators, through radio programs, mailings of flyers, and in particular, the magazine *Timón*, headed up by José Vasconcelos, the former Secretary of Education. Vasconcelos did not hide his sympathy with the Nazis: "The Mexican people may be largely Germanophile, and we believe that indeed they are; but the reason for this is precisely that they see in the rupture of contemporary international order a kind of liberation," he wrote. Dr. Atl, a painter famous throughout Mexico, considered Nazism to be the solution to global problems. In 1940, ex-revolutionary Adolfo León Osorio exhorted Mexico to expel all Jews, and although the government aligned itself with the US from 1939 onwards, most opinion leaders were openly against supporting Franklin D. Roosevelt.

The Nazi indoctrination did not reach the top of Mexican politics: the president of Mexico, Lázaro Cárdenas, a reformist with a leftist social program, an enemy of fascism, who had supported the republican regime in Spain through different means, opening the doors to many refugees and even receiving a shipment of 500 Spanish children who were "adopted" by Mexico to protect them from the horror of the war. Cárdenas himself posed for a photo with the young boys and girls. In 1938, when Germany annexed Austria, the *Anschluss*, Mexico was the only country in the world to officially protest before the League of Nations. With the beginning of the war in 1939, Mexico decided to remain neutral and continue this way as long as possible, since Germany, Italy and Japan had become important recipients of its exports.

There are reasons to suspect that the government of Lázaro Cárdenas (1934-1940) turned a blind eye to Nazi activity in Mexico and that at some point it tacitly backed the Germans while the official party line continued to support the US. The German consulate in Mexico was disseminating intense propaganda against the US, insistent that the Third Reich had no intention of disturbing the peace in Latin America. In a communiqué from the 18th of December 1940, the German government declared: "As the Führer and the German government have protested several times, the Third Reich is not pursuing any political interests or territorial aspirations on the American continent, and any claim to the contrary comes from Anglo-Saxon and Judaic sources, whose propaganda aims to undermine the good relations between Latin America and Germany and thus reinforce the economic dependency of Latin American countries on Anglo-Saxon plutocracy."

In the end, President Cárdenas symbolized the attitude of many Mexicans: keeping an open door for Germany, not because they supported or approved of Hitler's actions, but because of suspicion and distrust towards the United States. Finally, in 1940, the year of the presidential election, Cárdenas expelled the German ambassador Arthur Dietrich upon learning from the US that the diplomat had brought into Mexico a large quantity of propaganda with a view to distributing it there. Phrases such as "Hitler is God's broom, here to sweep from the face of the Earth all the evil that has accumulated over centuries" were found in magazines financed by Germany and collaborated with by Mexican artists and intellectuals.

According to journalist and researcher Juan Alberto Cedillo, "throughout Latin America there was great sympathy with the Nazis owing to the imperialist attitudes of the British and North Americans and to the fact that the atrocities wrought by Hitler were not known there until the end of the war".[1] Mexico only had reason to be alarmed until Hitler invaded the Soviet Union: given that the majority of opinion leaders were socialists, their affinity with the Axis Powers was immediately extinguished. A few months earlier, Mexico's Secretary of Foreign Affairs, Ezequiel Padilla, had warned Congress of the need to cooperate with the Allies, since if Nazi Germany ultimately triumphed, not only would there be a world order dominated by a hostile force, but indigenous and mestizo Mexicans would also be oppressed by the

---

[1] Cedillo, Juan Alberto. *Los nazis en México: Nuevas revelaciones sobre la infiltración de la Alemania nazi en México*, México, 2010: DeBolsillo, p. 90.

racist policies of the Third Reich. The Japanese attack on the US base at Pearl Harbor and its brutal occupation of the Philippines, with which Mexico had historic connections, tipped the scales of Mexican opinion definitively in favor of the Allies.

That same year, the new president, Manuel Ávila Camacho, a soldier who had fought in the Mexican Revolution and who was famously affable and polite, showed some teeth by arresting numerous Italians and Germans caught attempting to sink several boats in the Port of Tampico. In April 1941, nine Italian ships docked at Tampico and four German boats at Veracruz were seized. The bank accounts of the countries of the Axis were frozen, and the use of any language other than Spanish was prohibited on long-distance phone calls. That same year, when the situation in Europe seemed to foretell a German victory, Mexico signed agreements with the US that allowed the latter to use their air bases, as well as various economic agreements, including the sale of essential raw materials. Mexico's strategic oil began to be transported north, using the Italian ships confiscated at Tampico, re-christened with Mexican names. This agreement concerning fuel supply was to trigger grave repercussions and lead to Mexico declaring war on the Axis.

Germany attacks

The Japanese bombing of Pearl Harbor seemed to unite the Mexicans in a sense of indignation and fear of the Axis Powers, nudged along by US propaganda. However, an even greater impact was likely achieved by the assignation of popular ex-president Lázaro Cárdenas to the role of Head of Defense of the Pacific Coast: a sparsely-populated area with a number of Japanese immigrants. This was far from a symbolic posting or a mere populist manoeuvre: in December 1941, the Mexican army had intercepted communications from the Japanese Empire revealing a plot to invade Mexico through Sonora and enter the US from there. Ex-president Cárdenas cooperated closely with the Americans in the placement of radar on the western coast, while at the other end of the country, in the Gulf, oil deliveries were still being made to New York.

In the early hours of May 14th 1942, one of the decommissioned Italian ships, the *Lucifero*, renamed the *Potrero del Llano*, was intercepted by the German submarine *U-564* lying in wait off the coast of Florida. Reinhard Suhren, its German captain, saw the Italian flag painted and illuminated on the unescorted boat's hull –it was in fact a Mexican flag, whose colors are identical to those of Italy– but his suspicions were aroused by its location and movements, and he attacked and sank it. Germany had not declared hostile feelings towards Mexico per se, but they had given warnings any country supporting the US.

The *Potrero del Llano* was carrying six thousand tons of oil and thirty-five crew members, of whom thirteen died, including the captain, Lieutenant Gabriel Cruz Díaz; the rest were rescued by an American boat. Some Mexican newspapers incorrectly reported that the Germans had killed the survivors struggling in the water with a machine gun.

The deputy of the ship, Jorge Mancisidor, said of the rescue: "We were asleep, except for two or three of us who were on guard from midnight to four in the morning. Suddenly, we heard a huge explosion and the boat rocked violently. I jumped out of my bunk and realized that the bridge had disappeared, with twelve crew members left from the other side. The hole made by the torpedo was directly underneath the captain's bunk, causing the explosion to occur right where the fuel tank was and splitting the boat in half from bow to stern. Flames immediately shot up and turned our boat into a hellish pit of fire."

"The torpedo hit us on the starboard side, killing all the men on deck," recalled another of the crew, Ricardo Gallardo, in 1995. "It all happened too fast to be able to lower the lifeboats. Only those of us who could swim managed to save ourselves. Once I realized the boat was sinking, I ran down to stop the machines and the furnaces, because even though the ship was on fire, the propeller was still going round. I thought that when we jumped into the water, it might hit and kill us. Some of my colleagues couldn't save themselves, because the oil spilling into the sea was on fire, so the boat was completely surrounded by flames. I thought I was the only one who had got out, because I watched so many of my fellow crew die. Once I was away from the boat, I started to hear distant voices and whistle; I swam over to them and found a group of five men. We were in the water for hours; we were all terrified, especially of sharks. We were rescued at dawn by a US navy patrol boat."

Helmsman Faustino Toledo recalled in 2012: "The (rescue) boats would not approach because they were afraid they would be torpedoed too. We arrived in Miami almost naked, haggard, scared, hungry, not yet recovered from the tragic surprise. We did not know who had sunk us ".

News of the attack, and the accompanying arrival home of thirteen bodies of Mexican sailors, had a profound impact on the nation's morale. José Vasconcelos, former Secretary of Education, accused the government of having provoked Germany by placing the ship in US waters, and German propagandists quickly began to circulate the rumor that the ships had actually been sunk by the US in order to drag Mexico into conflict —a myth some Mexicans still believe to this day. President Ávila Camacho sent angry notes of protest to Germany, demanding an apology and compensation for the losses. Hitler ignored him.

Six days later, it became clear that the Third Reich had not made a mistake, nor had they committed a tactical error: on the 21st May, a second confiscated Italian ship, the *Genoano*, renamed *Faja de Oro*, was attacked by German submarine *U-106* by Hermann Rasch. The ship was sailing unescorted midway between Yucatán and Florida under Ramón Sánchez Mena. At four o'clock in the morning of the 21st May 1942, the *U-106* intercepted it, launching two torpedos. One of them hit the target, but failed to sink the boat. Twenty minutes later, during which time the desperate crew members battled to escape, a second torpedo delivered the coup de grace. The ship caught alight and sank to the bottom of the sea. The attack was observed by the crew of another German submarine, the *U-753*, but they did not intervene. Seven Mexican sailors were killed.

IN MEMORY OF THE POTRERO DEL LLANO: "REMEMBER THE 13TH OF MAY OF 1942."

"Mexico was highly contemptuous of that action," stated Fernando Nava, one of the last remaining survivors of FAEM, in 2015. "Back then, most Mexicans had Nazi leanings, but when we saw that they had attacked Mexico, people became furious." A contemporary report paints a different picture. In a confidential memo from June 3ʳᵈ 1942, George Messersmith, the US ambassador, expressed his concerns that they were losing the ideological battle in Mexico:

> "After the sinking of the *Potrero del Llano* there were rumors spread all over the country, and I am sorry to say not without effect, that we had sunk the vessel for the purpose of forcing Mexico into the war. Public opinion here is in a peculiar and somewhat apathetic state still, although there is a great change since the sinking of the *Potrero del Llano*... All this, however, does not increase the love of a good many Mexicans for us, for whom we are the gringos with all the characteristics they heretofore credited us with." [2]

The Gentleman President

President Ávila Camacho had had a long career, albeit neither particularly noteworthy nor heroic, in the national army, and he was prepared to respond to this provocation as only a true military man would. Ambassador Messersmith had hoped the sinking of the national ships would unite the Mexican people against Hitler, but there continued to be a sense of mistrust directed both at the Axis and at the US and Great Britain. Only three years before, these latter countries had inundated Mexico with threats. Over a century of problems with Americans had left a stain on public perception.

Nevertheless, the 45-year-old "gentleman president" was clear on what was best for the country. He addressed Congress and the nation on the night of May 28ᵗʰ 1942. Outside the Chamber of Deputies, a crowd was waiting to greet him, comprising mostly bureaucrats and other government workers who had been brought there, in accordance with prevalent

---

[2] Messersmith, G.S., Messersmith Papers Special Collection, University of Delaware Library, collection MSS 1509-00, 3ʳᵈ June 1942.

political practice at the time, to applaud him and display unconditional support for anything he said in the Chamber. Up and down the country, people sat by their radios, listening intently as his grave, emotionless voice declared war on the Axis Powers. The conflagration was coming to Mexico.

Addressing the congressmen, ex-presidents, members of the army, diplomatic correspondents and other personalities gathered there to listen, Ávila Camacho stressed that "face to face with such repeated onslaughts (...) a free people anxious to keep realities, we declare, as proposed by the Council of Secretaries of State and Chiefs of Autonomous Departments, assembled in this city on Friday the 22nd last, that as from that date a state of war exists between our country, and Germany, Italy and Japan." He then added: "Yes, war, with all its consequences. War, which Mexico desired to outlaw for all time from the methods of civilized existence, but which, in cases like this, and in the present state of world disorder, constitutes the only way of asserting our right to independence and of preserving unharmed the dignity of our Republic."

The president's address and the news of the sailors' deaths started a wave of patriotism. According to the memoirs of General Francisco L. Urquizo, ex-revolutionary and Secretary of Defense, on two occasions, volunteers turned up at military camps up and down the country demanding to be trained up and sent to fight; it was an unstoppable frenzy. "Every day, several civilians were turning up at military sites to receive training, and varying groups of blue- and white-collar workers were asking for military training. This enthusiastic fighting spirit was not only evident in Monterrey, but in small towns and on ranches. It was happening all over the country. Military camps had become a daily pilgrimage. Waves of volunteers would turn up, people who had jobs but who were coming before work to receive military training, which meant getting up before five o'clock in the morning". [3]

---

[3] Urquizo, Francisco Luis. *Tres de diana.* Ediciones SEC Coahuila, p. 99.

MANUEL ÁVILA CAMACHO

However, Germany was not losing sleep over Mexico's declaration of war. The Reich had bigger fish to fry than the armed forces of the Latin American nation, categorized in German documents as "a small country": their real concern was that Ávila Camacho might drag the rest of the subcontinent into the war. It was to that end that the "gentleman president" acted as he did. On Pan American Day 1942, in a speech broadcast on the radio to the entire continent, he said: "Our continent cannot assume a purely passive role, one of mere moral condemnation of these aggressors. Even those of us who are not at war must work as if a hidden menace were approaching: strengthening our resistance skills and perfecting the organization of our armies." Ávila Camacho was inciting all Latin America to unite against the Axis.

Hitler's reaction to Mexico's declaration was to prove more humiliating for the Mexican people than the sinking of the ships in the Gulf. When he heard about Camacho's pronouncement of hostility, Germany's Minister of Foreign Affairs, Joachim von Ribbentrop, wrote in a communiqué: "For the Axis to make such a fuss about issuing a joint declaration of war against a little country as Mexico, which is under the domination of the US, would be giving Mexico's actions more importance than it deserves, and might produce the opposite effect to that desired".[4] In other words, for Nazi Germany, Mexico was a pest to which it was not worth paying attention. However, the weak, proud country had been provoked, and their ruling classes intended to capitalize on the situation.

A poll in the magazine *Tiempo* carried out after the sinking of the ships revealed that 80% of Mexicans were in favor of their country declaring war. This represented a drastic change in opinion: before the incident, 60% had claimed that they were against entering into conflict against the Axis. Many young Mexicans began to volunteer to go to the European front. Had they known the secret plans of the Japanese, they might have preferred instead to go to the Pacific, which was exactly what the 201st Squadron was ultimately to do.

The Asian empire was displaying a hostile attitude towards Mexico, despite the fact that Mexico and Japan had never had a difficult relationship and that there had been a large Japanese community in the country since the 19th century. A communiqué from 1942 stated: "Mexico's participation in the war must be called rash and outrageous. All she did was crumple under American pressure. She declared war and exposed her long weakly defended coastline, commiting military blunder. Why she went over to the United States in this war, the outcome of which is already decided, is beyond our understanding. Heretofore, all nations that have become the puppets of the Anglo-Saxons have

---

[4] See Paz, María Emilia, *Strategy, Security, and Spies: Mexico and the U.S. as Allies in World War II*. USA: Penn State University Press, p. 143.

one by one been annihilated. Mexico has wished this same fate upon her own self, and sorry as we are to say it, is treading the same path".[5]

The providential ambassador

"Severiano Pérez, who works in the gasoline station in the town of San Andrés, was enjoying the evening on a plaza bench when he heard that Mexico was at war (...) [Severiano] responded automatically... "*Viva México*! Death to the gringos! *Viva la revolución*!" and the crowd chorused full blast: "Viva!". The yells fell apart in bewildered mutters, however, when the telegrapher...pushed through from inside the store, shouting "Idiots! Imbeciles! We're against Germany! ... Don't you understand the gringos are on our side?" On the other side of the crowd where the women were, an old, cracked voice cried "God preserve us!"...and then in a strange, startled tone, "Who would have ever told me that I would come to be praying for gringos...!"

Anita Brenner, *The Wind that Swept Mexico*

Beneath its tangle of legislation, between declaring war on the Axis and dispatching troops, Mexico was lobbying and negotiating with Congress for the authorization to send armed contingents abroad. This had no precedent in all of Mexico's one hundred and twenty years as an independent nation. They had never sent so much as one soldier overseas. The US regarded the Mexican army as useless, a political body of barely twenty thousand members created to uphold order, maintain roads and install telephone lines, not to take on powers such as Germany or Japan. The country owned but a handful of tanks and fifteen boats that could be used for military purposes, but with obsolete weaponry and no anti-submarine defense.

---

[5] Ibidem, p. 144.

Nevertheless, the US ambassador to Mexico, Messersmith, floated the idea that it was necessary to mobilize the Mexican armed forces –at first, in order that they could patrol the coasts at home, but later, to be sent to the front. This was less due to their being required to win the war and more because it was in Mexico's interests. Manuel Ávila Camacho was astute enough to realize that the victors would be those to write the history books. "Roosevelt prudently noted his counterpart's general lack of authority to back up his offer [to send Mexicans to participate in the fight against the Axis], and replied with technical assistance and more modern equipment. The truth was, the Mexican armed forces completely lacked any of the logistic assets necessary to maintain an army on an overseas campaign." [6] But the threat of Japanese invasion of Mexico via the Pacific was a very real one; if seemingly implausible in retrospect, at the time it appeared to loom close on the horizon, and the fearmongering of the Mexican press further unsettled the public.

From the pivotal year of 1942 onwards, Ambassador Messersmith, a fierce critic of the Nazis during his years of diplomatic service in Austria, became convinced that the close collaboration between Mexico and the US, and the military involvement of Latin America, was essential. Messersmith was known for having helped Albert Einstein leave Germany. He was also noted for his organizational and negotiating capacities – indeed, his embassy in Mexico during the war was one of the largest and most important diplomatic agencies of the US. February 1942 saw the formation of the first cross-border committee for the coordination of defensive actions on the Pacific coast, as well as the sale of military equipment to Mexico at preferential rates and the training of Mexican pilots at US bases. The ambassador reported that Mexico had three hundred men who could patrol the coasts of the Gulf and the Caribbean, as long as the US provided them with fighter planes.

---

[6] Andy Hooper, "Las Águilas Aztecas", in *The Drink Tank* number 300. USA, 2011.

AMBASSADOR GEORGE S. MESSERSMITH

Initially, this was the reasoning behind sending the men to receive training at Texan air bases; but in May that year, a group of high-ranking officers, among them the commander of the military zone of Monterrey and Major General Cristóbal Guzmán Cárdenas, went to President Ávila to tell him that they wished to fight in the war.

On June 26th and 27th 1942, Germany sunk three more Mexican ships: the *Tuxpan*, *Las Choapas*, and the *Oaxaca*, all transporting fuel to the US. The first two were sunk shortly after sailing from Veracruz, barely twenty-five miles from the coast and within just a few hours of each other. The pilot Luis Noriega Medrano was the captain of a squadron of six planes from the 2nd Regiment and had undergone a two-week course in the States. Noriega was flying over the Gulf when he saw the German submarine *U-129*, and dropped two bombs on it. He later reported having seen an oil spill in the ocean, but the German torpedo boat managed to make its getaway towards the coast of France. With a view to guarding the coasts of Baja California and the Gulf of Mexico, the US sent several trains of modern armory to the capital.

On the civic parade of Independence Day of that year, the Mexican people stood agape watching the new arsenal pass by; morale was boosted and Mexico was galvanized. In 1943, George Messersmith secured for himself something that had seemed impossible: a presidential meeting in Mexico. It was to be the second cross-border meeting in the history of the two countries. In public, Roosevelt offered a hand to Mexico —but extended the other, too, expecting to receive raw materials in return. Behind closed doors and without the knowledge of Mexico's Congress, a matter less strategic but perhaps ultimately more important was being discussed, one whose transcendence would far exceed that of any other agreement: the involvement of Mexicans on the battlefield. The first step in this process was the dispatching of a Mexican military delegation to North Africa. General Luis Alamillo Flores was assigned to head up this group, a general of the revolutionary era who had been serving as military representative in Washington.

Also in the group was Colonel Antonio Cárdenas Rodríguez, a highly experienced pilot, known for his goodwill flight between Mexico and the US. Cárdenas Rodríguez was to be a key player in the years to come. The purpose of the mission to Africa was to introduce the Mexican middle management with the realities of the war. The group left Washington in secret on 28th April 1943, arriving in Morocco in early May before going on to Tunisia. General Alamillo enlisted in the 5th Division of the United States Army, while Cárdenas, the pilot, partook in bombing missions in Sicily and Sardinia. A letter sent on May 22nd from General James H. Doolittle, a national aviation pioneer, to Colonel Antonio Cárdenas, expresses his satisfaction "that you have had the opportunity to go on bombing missions and are currently involved in our operations".[7] This was technically Mexico's first military expedition of the Second World War.

---

[7] Enrique Sandoval, *Historia Oficial de la Fuerza Aérea Expedicionaria Mexicana.* Secretaría de la Defensa Nacional, 1946, p. 581.

PILOT LUIS NORIEGA MEDRANO

When this small Mexican mission of men returned home in June of that year, General Alamillo presented to Ávila Camacho his optimistic report of the situation, insisting that he allowed them to participate in the conflict in Europe as he was sure that they could have an important role to play. In the American press, the new generation of soldiers were complaining of being hindered by old generals of the Revolution who did not want to be overshadowed. The Mexican army as a whole fizzed with the desire to spring into action.

ANTONIO CÁRDENAS RODRÍGUEZ, 201st SQUADRON
COMMANDER

II. THE MEXICAN EXPEDITIONARY AIR FORCE

"When I suggested, therefore, that the first collaboration
should be in the form of a training squadron of the Mexican Air Force
in the United States for participation at some front, the President
accepted this idea very readily and said that he thought it was an
excellent one."

George Messersmith, American ambassador in 1942

In the early 1940s, Mexico was a society under reconstruction. It was experiencing its first promising few years in a long time: no civil war, no overthrows, no rebellious generals. The majority of the population lived in rural communities, but a middle class was beginning to form, and with it an urban culture. Mexico City was entering a period of rapid growth. Traditionally beautiful in its architecture, it displayed its newfound importance in monuments such as the Diana the Huntress Fountain and the *Monumento a la Raza*. In this hitherto disorganized country, radio had staked its claim in people's homes, forging a sense of national unity – perhaps even more so than the railways had done fifty years earlier. Cinema was in its prime, Mexican music and arts were blossoming, and for the first time, a national identity to which almost everyone could relate was being shaped. Agustín Lara,

Diego Rivera, Siqueiros, Dolores del Río and Cantinflas became household names.

Life in the cities was peaceful for the first time in years, with no hint of uprising. The economy was beginning to recover, although the initial effects of the war manifested in Mexico as shortages of basic products; but for most people, the horrors of Europe were but a distant rumor. When it became clear that the conflict had reached a global level and that the American continent would have to take a stance, the US created the Office of the Coordinator of Inter-American Affairs, to produce and distribute propaganda materials in Latin America. Mexican cartoonist (born in the city of Aguascalientes, in the writing central plateau) Antonio Arias Bernal was one of the first to lampoon Hitler in his weekly vignettes.

Arias Bernal took aim at Hitler, Mussolini and Emperor Hirohito at a time at which Mexican politicians were ignoring the Führer and many intellectuals were even dabbling in Nazism. The caricutarist perceived a tendency in propaganda to divide the continent, so from 1938 onwards, his sketches displayed Panamerican themes. Despite not yet having knowledge of the atrocities occurring in Europe, Arias Bernal, born in the city of Aguascalientes, appeared to understand the danger posed by the Third Reich. Three years prior to Mexico declaring war on Germany, the artist was mocking Hitler in his cartoons to the point that he received threatening letters.[8] His conviction attracted the attention of the Office of the Coordinator of Inter-American Affairs in the States, and they offered him work.

The cartoonist aimed his work at boosting public morale. Six million copies were made of each of the first twelve sketches he produced in the US. His poster *As One Man in the Pacific* dramatized imaginary battles between Nazis and Mexican *charros*; it derided Hitler and his followers, thus lessening their capacity to incite fear.

---

[8] "Mexican Cheered by War Spirit Here", *The New York Times*, 2nd October 1942, pp. 23.

CARTOON BY ANTONIO ARIAS BERNAL, ONE OF FEW
MEXICANS WHO RECOGNISED THE NAZI THREAT AT THE
TIME.

Arias depicted Churchill and De Gaulle as legendary heroes. "Until Arias Bernal went to Washington," Margarita Nelken would later go on to write in the magazine *Hoy*, "propaganda, attempting to foment fear of the enemy, only served to glorify them. The intuition of Arias Bernal swapped that impression of chilling monstrosity for one of absurdity: a thousand times more effective." As *Life* magazine put it, Arias Bernal waged his private war on Hitler.

And so it was that the work of this cartoonist, a Mexican combatant like any other —albeit one who wielded a pencil rather than a rifle— came to be in such demand that copies were even distributed from the air over Nazi-occupied France.[9] The Office of the Coordinator of Inter-American Affairs, under Nelson Rockefeller, was so influential that Walt Disney produced a movie aimed at fostering a sense of unity. *The Three Caballeros* debuted in Mexico City in the run-up to Christmas 1944. Part animation and part live-action with artists of the era, the film showed Donald Duck and two of his friends, Mexican fighting cock Pancho Pistolas and Brazilian parrot José Carioca. At the suggestion of Miguel Moreno Arreola a year later, the former became the mascot of the 201st Squadron.

Another American initiative created to foster this sense of unity across the continent was the dispatching of Latin American troops to the front, albeit on a token scale. Messersmith pitched the idea directly to General Marshall, Chief of Staff of the US army, and General Henry Arnold of the Air Force. Once these men were in agreement, they elevated the matter to President Roosevelt: Mexico could send a single air contingent, made up of the most experienced and reliable pilots they could find, to be trained by the US Air Force.[10] However, there were to be several

---

[9] Gustavo Vázquez Lozano, *El siglo XX en la mirada de Arias Bernal*, ICA, 2007.

[10] Brazil, eager to mend fences with the US, also took part in WWII, although less symbolically than Mexico: President Getúlio Vargas sent 25,000 land and sea troops to fight in Italy and the Battle of the Atlantic.

further meetings between Messersmith, President Ávila Camacho and the Mexican Secretary for Foreign Affairs, Ezequiel Padilla, before the green light could be given and the details agreed upon. Meanwhile, the alliance was treated with the utmost caution and secrecy. In 1943, a reporter from *The New York Herald Tribune* asked Lázaro Cárdenas, the Secretary of War, if the country would be participating; the ex-president responded: "With what weapons? With arrows? With stones? Mexico has none of the equipment necessary for modern warfare."

Nevertheless, Ávila Camacho understood that only those countries that had fought against the Axis would have any voice in post-war negotiations or even redistribution. Sending a single air squadron would be beneficial for both nations. Had Mexico elected to send infantry, the minimum would have to be at least one Division; that is, fifteen thousand men, whose actions would have been wiped out against the colossal size of the Allies. An air squadron, on the other hand, could comprise just thirty pilots. For Mexico, this would be a symbolic number under the orders of the US army. A higher number might have offended public sensibilities, and any more losses might have destroyed the political capital of President Ávila Camacho. In addition, during the Second World War, the number of casualties in air squadrons was significantly fewer than those in land-based units, as demonstrated in the case of Brazil.

Ambassador Messersmith met President Roosevelt for a second time in early 1944 in order to inform him of the Mexican situation. Since war had been declared, he told him, Mexican generals were keen to join in the combat. However, Messersmith was of the opinion that Mexico was not ready, and that the best option would be to deploy one to three air squadrons. He also told him that Mexico's involvement would be more for political ends than out of necessity. President Roosevelt picked up the phone and asked to meet with General Henry Arnold, the head of the Air Force. Messersmith received instructions to meet with the Mexican president and inform him that the involvement of one to three air squadrons would be well-received by the US. [11]

For the Allies, at this advanced stage in the war, the situation in Europe was already decided. Roosevelt and his generals knew that the action would be centered around the Pacific, where mobility, speed, lethality, and efficacy were required against targets far removed from each other before an enemy in retreat. Weeks later, the indefatigable Messersmith wrote in a confidential memo: "The following brief paragraph is one that cannot be used in any published notes, but as a matter of interest I wish to record the following here...President Roosevelt himself mentioned [the participation of a Mexican squadron] to me and said: "Where are we going to send them?" I told President Roosevelt that President Ávila Camacho had great admiration for General McArthur. He had met General McArthur some years before when General McArthur had made a visit to Mexico. He often spoke of him in very glowing terms. [McArthur] spoke of [Ávila Camacho] in somewhat the same terms...The President [Roosevelt] said that it was wonderful and that he would telegraph himself to General McArthur. I do not know the nature of the telegrams which passed between the President and General McArthur, but it was very shortly thereafter that the President informed me that the (Mexican) squadron would go to fight under the command of General McArthur. When I mentioned this to President Ávila Camacho he was tremendously pleased". [12]

The air show: March 5th 1944

Back home, the Gentleman President was facing two problems: convincing the public that it was in the country's interests to send young men to fight against the Axis, and doing so sufficiently delicately that Congress would not suspect that the decision had

---

[11] Messersmith, G.S., *Messersmith Papers Special Collection*, University of Delaware Library, collection MSS 1580. 17th February 1944.

[12] Messersmith, G.S., *Messersmith Papers Special Collection*, University of Delaware Library, collection MSS 109, ID number 2031-00. Undated.

already been made and that several pilots were already undergoing training in Texas.

In March of 1944, the old Department of Aviation, which had three squadrons in service, was officially transformed into the Mexican Air Force, increasing the number of squadrons to ten: the *101, 201, 202, 203, 204, 205, 206, 207, 208* and *209*. On March 5th an air show took place on the outskirts of Mexico City for one hundred thousand amazed onlookers living in the capital. Several AT-6 and A-24B fighter planes simulated the bombing of an enemy base. The show, which was a roaring success, was principally aimed at demonstrating to the Mexican people the level which the pilots had reached, as well as bolstering confidence in the newly-created Mexican Air Force and selling the idea that Mexico could, after all, kick Hitler's and Emperor Hirohito's behinds, just like in the cartoons of Arias Bernal.

Ávila Camacho and his entire cabinet were there to watch the display. It was obvious that something was afoot, although newspapers of the time continued to insist that Mexico would not be sending soldiers to the fighting front. On March 8th, at a private dinner with the Air Force, the President told those present that "no one is more suitable to fly our national flag than the Air Force". On March 15th, Messersmith officially presented Mexico's offer to Roosevelt. In early July, negotiations were finalized in Mexico City with the visit of Colonel L.C. Ryan to the Secretary of Defense. Mexico sent half a million dollars to the States to defray a portion of the costs: a token amount. Three important agreements were reached: that no member of the squadron was to wear a US emblem, that they would receive orders from their Mexican commander only, and that they would be subject only to Mexican martial law. President Ávila also requested that the place to which they were being dispatched not be mentioned. The Mexican Expeditionary Air Force (FAEM) was to comprise three hundred people, of whom ten per cent would be pilots and the remainder would be land-based staff: meteorologists, mechanics, medics, radio operators, cooks, and draftsmen. They were to present themselves before July 25th at Randolph Fields, Texas.

From there, they would be sent to varying locations for training, which would last three months; a very short time, but the war made matters pressing. Not only was it the first time Mexico was to declare war on another country, but the Berlin-Rome-Tokyo Axis was a force infinitely more powerful and ruthless than the United States. Compared to Nazi Germany and imperial Japan, Mexico´s previous clashes with the US had been mere neighborly squabbles. [13]

The sister country

The decision to deploy the 201st Squadron for combat in the Philippines –so named in honor of King Philip II of Spain– had a symbolic value, and, for the Mexicans, an air of legitimacy: the two countries had ethnic, cultural, and linguistic connections, and many surnames in common. This was the legacy of the Mexican and Spanish colonial presence, and the countries had a shared history of the more than three hundred years during which the Far East colony was governed from New Spain. Thousands of Mexicans had stayed in the Philippines, and many more in the country were of Filipino descent, particularly on the Pacific coast. So tightly-woven were the two countries for centuries that many Nahuatl words were adopted by the Filipinos.

Until the early twentieth century, Spanish was the language commonly used on the islands, although when Japan invaded the archipelago, it was already falling out of favor. However, the high-ranking officials and the cultural elite in Manila continued to use it. The archipelago, comprising over seven thousand islands, was occupied by the Japanese Empire from the middle of 1942, and the conditions imposed by Hirohito on the Filipino people were known throughout Mexico. These included war crimes, interminable atrocities, slave camps and civilian massacres. Philippine President Manuel L. Quezón had visited Mexico and

---

[13] As well as Nazi Germany, the Japanese empire also committed massacres and enslaved the civil population in occupied territories, particularly in the Philippines.

the United States in 1937, desperate at the Japanese imperial expansion, and although he was basically ignored in the north, in Mexico he had received a warm welcome and made friends with then Secretary of War, Manuel Avila Camacho.

So Mexico may have felt mistrust towards the US, but the liberation of the Philippines was a cause Mexicans could wholeheartedly embrace. General Arthur R. Harris, military attaché in México, informed his country that Mexico was becoming impatient with Washington's slowness to dispatch its troops to the fighting front.

> "They (the Mexicans) are becoming impatient and a little dismayed at the apparent coolness in which their patriotic and unselfish offer has been received. It should be emphasized that the Mexican is a very sensitive and proud individual. He takes offense very easily at any slight, even when it is slight only by implication. I believe that there is a real danger than unless there is some notice taken of the President of Mexico's offer of troops that the war spirit among the higher officials will perceptibly cool." [14]

In the same communiqué, Harris expressed approval for the choice of the Philippines as a destination:

> "In past conversations with Mexican officers, I have heard the thought expressed that if Mexico ever sent troops abroad, they should go to the South Pacific, especially the Philippines where the Mexicans' knowledge of guerrilla fighting, their familiarity with jungles and mountains, also the fact that they speak Spanish, could all be used most advantageously."

---

[14] Stephen I. Schwab. "The Role of the Mexican Expeditionary Air Force in World War II: Late, Limited, but Symbolically Significant." *The Journal of Military History*, Vol. 66, No. 4 (Oct., 2002), p. 1125.

With negotiations at an end, perhaps the most surprising symbolic act of collaboration between the countries occurred: a high-profile achievement that no generation of Mexicans could have ever envisaged in their wildest dreams. On the night of September 15th 1944, the eve of Mexican Independence celebrations, Generals Joseph McNamey and Henry Pratt joined the president of Mexico in his traditional re-enactment of the call to arms from the balcony of the National Palace. Under the fireworks and to the sound of the *mariachi* band, nobody suspected that, far out of public earshot, the Mexican government was following US orders and demanding that governors of the states seized the properties of Japanese immigrants –peace-abiding citizens who had lived in the country for generations– and sent them to detention centers in Guadalajara and Mexico City. General Lázaro Cárdenas, who had just one year previously disparaged the ability Mexican army to take part in the Second World War –invoking the ire of many other generals– declared then that "Mexican troops should have the chance to participate in combat, because after this war, no country that has not given its all will be able to hold its head up high. While I once claimed that men armed with sticks and stones could not take part in a modern war, thanks to the generosity of the United States and the work of the Defense Committee, the Mexican army is now reasonably well-equipped with modern weaponry, and we have worked hard to train them well."

Recruitment and selection

Pilot selection began in 1944. The strongest candidates floated to the top among aviation academy graduates. Many of them had had scholarships in the US. "Competition, even for the support positions," writes Andy Hooper, "was fierce. Armorers, mechanics, clerks, cooks, drivers… A series of examinations were held, and these were used to select the final candidates. Because the education needed to become an aviator was mostly available to upper-class students, most of the pilots were from aristocratic families.[15] But the decisions were made on merit, and there were a few foundlings and orphans mixed with the fortunate sons." Miguel Moreno Arreola recalled for the *Los Angeles Times* in 2004: "I was a very humble boy. I was an orphan. I didn't get there because I was privileged. I earned it, and I wanted to help. They were all upper-class, but I was very proud of myself. I was self-made."

The volunteers came from both the northern and southeastern states of Mexico; from cities such as Mexico City and Guadalajara, from towns and ranches. Most had graduated from the governmental aviation school, some had already trained for many hours in the US, and almost all had at least rudimentary English. A few members of the squadron had patrolled the Mexican coasts in 1942 and 1943. Among the land-based staff, there was a young man who had worked as a reporter for the English-language newspaper the *Mexico City Herald*, an armorer who had studied in Paraguay, and a cook from a patisserie in Mexico City. A notable case was that of Manuel Alcántar Torres, a Mexican who had fought with the American army in Casablanca and Sicily and had requested his honorable discharge in order to enlist in the Mexican Expeditionary Air Force.

Reynaldo Pérez Gallardo, of San Luis Potosí, was the son of a governor and had an impeccable military history. He had studied at a boarding school in San Antonio where he had learned English, and had been interested in planes since he was a boy. "Instead of going to school, I would go to the San Luis Potosí airfield", he remembered for the VOCES-Oral History Project at the University of Texas. "Back then, planes would get dirty underneath, their underbelly. They would get dirty with oil and I used to volunteer to clean them in exchange for a little ride

---

[15] Not all branches of the army were in agreement to participate in the war. In 1944, an attempt was made on the President's life –from which he escaped unhurt– by a soldier. On July 10th there was an attempted coup d'etat under Captain Benito Castañeda Chavarría, due to a rumour that ten thousand Mexican soldiers were to be sent to the front. Castañeda was sentenced to death, but Ávila Camacho gave him a presidential pardon.

around the airport onboard one of those planes at the end of the day."

Miguel Moreno Arreola had been raised by a priest, and later in an orphanage. He was too poor to pay for higher education tuition and did not have the contacts needed to obtain a scholarship. At the age of twenty, he enrolled in military school, attracted by the $2.50 pesos it offered per week. During his years there, he met the famous pilot Francisco Sarabia, a Mexican aviation pioneer. With hard work and dedication, Moreno rose up the ranks of the rigid military structure and was selected to be a member of the 201st. Fortino González Gudiño worked in an armory of the Mexican army, making grenades. There was an accidental explosion and Fortino went inside to rescue two persons who were trapped, risking his life. This gained him his superiors´ recognition and a place to go to war. Javier Martínez Valle had arrived with his father in Mexico City looking for his mother. On the way to the meeting, his father was hit by a truck and lost his life. Martínez Valle was left wandering around the city when he reached the location of the film *Hell Divers* (1931) starring Wallace Berry, which was being filmed at the time in the capital. When he recounted his tragedy, the young man got a job with the filming crew. This was his first contact with military aviation. He later enrolled in the Military College and the Aviation School, where he was selected for the squadron thanks to his knowledge of English and because he had worked as a mechanic at the airport.

The pilots selected to go for training were mostly taken from the existing 201st Squadron of the Mexican Air Force, although some came from other squadrons and divisions of the army. Geographically speaking, the country was well-represented. Ramiro Bastarrachea Gamboa came from the town of Tizpéhual, Yucatán; Pedro Martínes de la Concho, a mechanic, had come from Baja California; radio operator Pedro Ramírez Corona from a town in Colima; "Miguel Alcantar Torres, a paratrooper with U.S. combat experience at Casablanca, Bizerte and Sicily, received an honorable discharge from the U.S. Army to join; Joaquín

Ramírez Vilchis, a pilot and scion of a prominent Mexico City family, had commanded a cavalry unit in Jalisco. All were eager to serve with the elite FAM." [16] In terms of age, two generations were sent alongside each other. One member, Reynaldo Gallardo, was sixteen years old when Mexico declared war on the Axis. Lieutenant José Espinosa Fuentes was twenty-two as was Second Lieutenant Fausto Vega Santander. Heading up the Mexican Expeditionary Air Force was Major General Antonio Cárdenas Rodríguez, born in 1903 in Sonora; at the time of the formation of the Squadron, he was forty-one.

Antonio Cárdenas had extensive military experience and had been a pioneer of Mexican aviation. As a member of the army, he had participated in bombings against the Yaqui Native Americans in Sonora and later against Cristero forces in central Mexico. Before the country had declared war on the Axis, he had served as head of the further education group in the US. Interestingly, it did not escape the FBI's notice that, in 1934, Cárdenas had made a number of visits to Japan on which "the Japanese Government and high Japanese naval officers lavishly entertained him". Some US intelligence officials protested against his appointment as leader of the FAEM. [17] In the early 1940s, Cárdenas Rodríguez had flown as an observer with US forces in Italy and North Africa. This regarding the command of the 300-member Mexican Expeditionary Air Force. In charge of the 30 pilots of the 201st Squadron was an experienced young aviator named Radamés Gaxiola Andrade, a distant relative of Francisco I. Madero, son of a Mexican general of the Revolution, and a military college graduate with over three thousand flying hours on American planes. Gaxiola had been to primary school in Los Angeles, graduating from military college in Mexico and later the Air Force in 1939. He had taken legendary pioneer Gustavo Salinas —the

---

[16] Mexican Air Force Helped Liberate the Philippines, in *Aviation History*, 12th June 2006.

[17] Jerry García, *Looking Like the Enemy: Japanese Mexicans, the Mexican State, and US Hegemony, 1897–1945*. USA: University of Arizona Press, 2014, p. 148.

first Mexican to use a plane to bomb a target, during the Mexican Revolution— to Europe to observe the war.

The long road to the USA

In July, the 201st Squadron was ready to begin training. Up to that point, the team's objective and target were a state secret. The official line was that they were going on a training mission. Only four people in Mexico knew the true motive: they were President Ávila, the Secretary of Foreign Affairs, the Chief of the Mexican Air Force, and Secretary of War Lázaro Cárdenas. Their first stop was to be an army camp near San Antonio, Texas, where the hardest part of the training would take place. Before they departed, President Ávila Camacho and General Lázaro Cárdenas inspected the members of the Squadron in front of a warplane at the army camp of Balbuena, near to the site from which Mexico's first planes had taken off. In his official farewell, the president let slip the true nature of the mission, exactly what the pilots had been wanting. "The war has not reached our coasts," said Ávila Camacho, "but Mexico has a duty as an ally of the countries fighting for freedom. We must be prepared for any eventuality."

After Ávila Camacho reminded them that their brothers in the Republic of Brazil would also be aiding them, he invited the soldiers, possibly simply as protocol, to "inform me of any problem they may have or any request they may wish to make of me." Before the ceremony, the soldiers had been warned not to "ask anything" of the president. Even so, one of the members of the group took two steps forward, saluted, and said in a loud, clear voice: "Mister President, I am Corporal Ángel Bocanegra del Castillo. Sir, I request that a school is built in my town of Tepoztlán, Morelos."

The group of brave men were given a noteworthy sendoff at Buenavista station in Mexico City; the town had never seen such a turnout. As in other countries, the newspapers printed scenes of mothers kissing their sons on the cheeks and holding back tears, and girlfriends less able to hide their sorrow. *Las Golondrinas*, a

Mexican farewell song, rang throughout the streets. For some, this was truly to be their last goodbye. The men's trip north, which should have taken them no longer than a day, lasted six, because the train pulled into every town so the people could celebrate their heroes with music, flags and hugs. They made stops in Saltillo and Monterrey. On July 26th in Nuevo Laredo, the last station, the Squadron was greeted with cheers from the townspeople and by opportunistic politicians who had flown in to have their photo taken with the troops. At sundown, the train crossed the border. Its passengers were struck by the sudden silence and solitude: "There was no one there," recalled one veteran, years later.

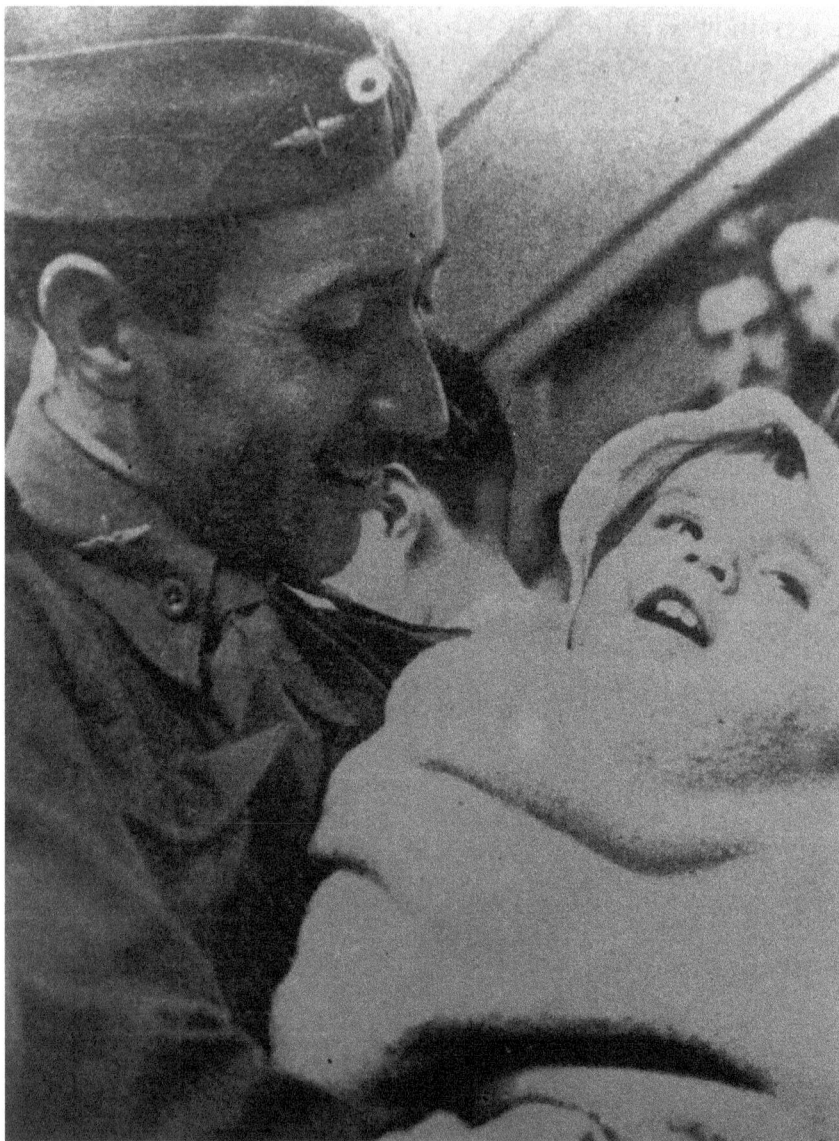

FAREWELLS OF THE MEXICAN EXPEDITIONARY AIR
FORCE, BUENAVISTA STATION,
JULY 24TH 1944.

III. TRAINING OF THE 201ST SQUADRON

"I know how enthusiastic you all were when it came to applying to form part of this Squadron. There were not enough places for everyone. You who are here were lucky enough to be selected, and for that you should be proud. When you leave, you will have no concerns other than your families. But you need not worry; we will watch over them."

Manuel Ávila Camacho, to the members of the 201st Squadron

The first stop was at the Randolph Field airbase in San Antonio, Texas. From there, the three hundred members of the FAEM were sent to various cities for different types of training: there were mechanics, draughtsmen, medics, and, of course, the thirty fighter pilots. Testimonies differ regarding the manner in which they were received in the US. Fernando Nava recalls: "They told us 'This is where you're camping'. We thought they were going to give us somewhere to sleep, but that night we slept on the floor." The following morning, they rose early, hoisted the Mexican flag on US territory, and played the national anthem on a record player Nava himself had brought with him. Miguel Moreno Arreola remembers it as "the most moving thing I have ever experienced. How I cried! It was so beautiful."

However, the men soon realized that racism was alive and kicking in Texas, and Mexicans were not held in high regard. Hispanic people living there were viewed alongside African

Americans as third-class citizens. In a store in Greenville, a US officer requested that the owner removed from the window a sign reading "*No Mexicans, no Dogs*". Another establishment carried the slightly less offensive but equally provocative "*Greenville: Welcome to the Blackest Land, the Whitest People*". A few members of the Squadron were dumbfounded when they were refused service in a café, and some found it difficult to find lodgings, since it was hotel policy in Greenville not to accept Catholics, black people or "Yankees", that is to say, people from the north. Also, recruits from Latin American countries, including Mexico, misinterpreted the tough manner of the military chiefs and endured the superiority of some others. In particular towards Mexicans, "special difficulty arose (...) because of its location in an area where prejudice towards Latin Americans was widespread."[18]

Some US troops viewed the Mexicans with suspicion, doubtful that they had the ability to pilot a warplane. There was also a language barrier; the Americans did not have much Spanish, nor could the members of the 201st Squadron communicate well in English. No one appeared to have taken this matter seriously up until that point, and the situation became so complicated that a special unit of translators known as "Section 1" had to be created, headed up by Captain Paul B. Miller, who had served for many years in Peru. The committee taught technical terms related to aviation and thus facilitated communication to such an extent that the squadron was able to integrate into the 58th fighting group of the 5th Air Force.

After their reception at Randolph, the Mexicans were separated into smaller groups in order to receive training at varying bases: San Antonio, Victoria and Majors Field (Texas); Pittsburg (California); and Camp Stoneman in Pocatello (Idaho), which was where the largest group was sent. Upon their arrival, high-ranking army officers handed them a Mexican flag, Spanish-

---

[18] Thomas H. Greer, "Other Training Programs," in *The Army Air Forces in World War II*, Volume 6 of "Men and Planes", Washington: Office of Air Force History, 1983, pp. 699.

language movies were shown on the projector, and the pilots were allowed to celebrate public holidays. However, weather conditions in Idaho were so adverse that they were forced to transfer once again to Texas, further delaying their training. The instructors were uninterested in educating those whom they viewed as a burden; a mere product of political negotiations. In the end, a large part of the training was delivered by female pilots, known as WASPs: Women's Air Service Pilots. In turn, ground crew – mechanics, armorers, radio operators, and so on– were sent to other training centers in the States.

POCATELLO, IDAHO

In February 1944, seven Mexican pilots were dispatched to the Naval Air Station North Island, San Diego. Their mission was to fly the Douglas A-24B in a squadron that specialized in dive bombing. Eight A-24B aircraft from the US were painted with the emblem of the Mexican Air Force, and they formed their own separate squadron. In charge of the group was Captain Carlos

Cervantes Pérez, and the pilots were Carlos Garduño Núñez, Fernando Hernández Vega, Graco Ramírez Garrido, Julio Cal, Crisóforo Salido and Jacobo Estrada Luna. In mid-March of 1944, Colonel Antonio Cárdenas Rodríguez took over the entire training program.

To console themselves over their somewhat indifferent treatment, particularly in Texas, the Squadron encouraged camaraderie, forming a store-club known as "El Acuario" where they would meet during their free time and exalt their wounded national pride. They named themselves the *Águilas Aztecas* –the Aztec Eagles– and, at the suggestion of Miguel Moreno Arreola, they adopted Pancho Pistolas, a character from the Disney movie *The Three Caballeros*, as their mascot. One member of the group, Ángel Sánchez Rebollo, was even intrepid enough to begin courting an American teenager living in Victoria, Texas, by the name of Nancy Hudson. Her parents forbade her from seeing him, but the couple eloped to Brownsville. The marriage lasted until Nancy's death in 1986.

Crisis of command and death

The training period was peppered with challenges and losses. Uncertainty over whether they would ever make it to the fighting front hung over the men, and there was even a crisis at command level. Antonio Cárdenas, the leader of the three hundred members of the FAEM, was suspected of harboring pro-Japanese sentiment. The Americans were openly hostile towards Cárdenas and at one point attempted to have him replaced by Colonel Eliseo Martín del Campo. The matter made its way to the ears of the National Palace in Mexico City. Exasperated, President Ávila Camacho ratified him as leader of the FAEM.

It is likely that their naturally jovial disposition led many Mexicans to underestimate the mutual tension and mistrust, and those who did realize it, glossed over it. "[In Pocatello, Idaho] we won the townspeople over and earned their trust," recalled Manuel Cervantes Ramos. "We were constantly being invited to stay at their homes. The song *Bésame Mucho* by Consuelo Velázquez had reached them there, and people were interested in Latino music." Since the language barrier was proving a hindrance, English language lessons were added to the training program, although towards the end of the year the issue became less pressing since enough American instructors with good Spanish had been appointed.

In late November of 1944, the Squadron finally received their Republic P-47 Thunderbolt fighter planes for practicing combat techniques at thirty-five thousand feet. The Mexican pilots received training involving one hundred and twenty hours of air combat, attacking and escorting warships, dive bombing, navigating with instruments through poor weather, nighttime flying in formation, bombing ships while flying at sea level, producing smokescreens and navigating unknown waters.

BRIEFING AT THE CAMP

"We had eagerly awaited the formidable P-47 aircraft," remembered Colonel Joaquín Ramírez Vilchis. "They had told us that these planes were the big guns, for real men, and we were so excited seeing the huge machines landing in Pocatello, with their mighty engines roaring as they taxied down the runways. But to our surprise, we saw that the pilots delivering these planes to us... were women."

The P-47 Thunderbolt was not a new fighter plane nor was it the most important craft in the US in the spring of 1945, but up until two years previously it had been one of the main players in battles on the European front. It was still an excellent aircraft for combat against anything that they could face in the skies above the Pacific, thanks to the great altitudes it could reach, although its excessive tonnage had caused several accidents. The Americans called it "The Jug" because of the shape of its fuselage; the Mexicans christened it "El Jarro" or "El Pecuas" (short for P-47 as pronounced in Spanish). The Mexicans used the D model of the *Jarro*, with improved submachine guns, fuel tanks and fuselage, plus a bubble-shaped cabin that allowed for 360-degree vision. When diving, it could reach the speed of sound.[19] The disadvantage was the P-47 could only carry one passenger, so members had to learn to fly solo. Within just two weeks, English was being used for all radio transmissions, except in emergencies, where a bilingual Mexican pilot would interpret.

Although Paul B. Miller, 24, was the highest authority at the site, and later Colonel Arthur Kellog, all orders came from Major Radamés Gaxiola Andrade, who was at the forefront of most bombing missions. The general high morale of the Mexicans led to another incident which jeopardized the career of one of the pilots of the Squadron, when he flew his P-47 only a few meters above the main street of Greenville, the aircraft's wings almost touching the rooftops and sparking panic among the townspeople. The pilot, Gallardo, was immediately suspended by Captain Miller and reassigned as a mechanic. "It helped me a lot, because I learned so much," he said. "I was in charge of land-based services. I was sad, but I knew one day I would fly again." He was reintroduced to the group of pilots some time later.

---

[19] Haro, Dany. *The Forgotten Eagles* (Documentary). Directed by Víctor Mancilla. US: 201 Productions, 2006.

As time went on, with the war in Europe coming to an end and their training proving interminable, the members of the Squadron began to wonder if anything they were doing would ultimately be useful, or if they were simply pawns. Germany was on its knees, Italy had already fallen, and it seemed clear that there was no call for sending a squadron of inexperienced Mexicans to Berlin. "It was obvious that there wasn't going to be time to be part of the action in Europe," observed Captain Amadeo Castro Almanza. "Hitler's armies were in the early stages of defeat." Public opinion in Mexico was that it would be unhelpful and dangerous to send Mexican men to fight in a war that was already won; particularly because President Ávila Camacho, delighted by the population's high regard for the 201st Squadron, was showing signs of wanting to send ground troops to Europe. It was too late. But Japan had not capitulated yet, and it seemed that the War of the Pacific could be Mexico's last chance saloon. "We thought [that we would be sent to the Pacific] because of the type of training that we had begun to receive since our fighting squadron was established, and because of the equipment we received." [20]

The end of training

The training program, which should have finished in early November 1944, had been extended to February of the following year. All was not going well. One pilot, Crisóforo Salido Grijalva, died during practice. He had been attempting takeoff on a taxiway (also known as wheel track and not suitable for takeoff) at Major's Field, Texas, while preparing to practice machine-gunning with a camera, mission number fifty-eight of the program. Unaware that he was going down a taxiway, Salido Grijalva realized too late that he did not have enough runway to lift off, despite the shouts of his fellow pilots. The aircraft lurched nose-first into a swamp. The

---

[20] Along with Mexico, seventeen other Latin American countries sent staff to the US to be trained by the Air Force; however, only Brazil and Mexico joined in the action. The air squadron from Brazil was assigned to the Mediterranean.

pilot died instantly, inside the cabin. He was the first casualty of the 201st Squadron, and they had not yet left the United States.

Two of the pilots who passed their exams were, after a brief stay at Foster Field, deemed not suitable for flight and discharged for return to Mexico; all the remaining pilots passed. The Mexicans achieved results considered "very good, above average" over their one hundred and twenty obligatory flying hours divided into five stages.

COLONEL ANTONIO CÁRDENAS RODRÍGUEZ,
LEADER OF THE FAEM

"The pilots demonstrated their flying ability, and during the first week, all except one were approved to [fly] the P-47. Major Miller determined that the young pilots of the 201st Squadron were 'significantly above average' in terms of judgment, technique, takeoff, landing and general performance. In December 1944, he also reported that the general proficiency of the Mexicans was excellent and that their formation flying ranged from excellent to superior." [21] The most outstanding pilot, according to the official

---

[21] Retrieved May 15th 2017 from

scoring sheet, was Second Lieutenant Raúl García Mercado, with a score of 17.8% hits when firing in the air, and 30.3% hits on ground targets. The second most outstanding was the squadron leader, Radamés Gaxiola, with 28.5% hits on ground targets. The pilot with the highest score for in-air shots was Lieutenant Carlos Varela with 24%. Some pilots achieved just 1% hits. In total, the pilots accumulated over a thousand flying hours throughout their training, with an average of thirty-one hours per pilot at the airbases at Pocatello and Major's Field.

At Christmas, high-ranking officers of the Mexican army visited the members of the FAEM to deliver presents sent by their families. Before the year's end, the Mexican senate finally authorized the president to dispatch troops abroad. The news was gratefully received by the three hundred members of the FAEM, as up until that point, they had been training with no certainty that they would ever have the opportunity to put into practice the knowledge they were acquiring.

The members of the 201st Squadron attended their graduation ceremony on February 22nd 1945, accompanied by Mexico's Undersecretary of Defense, Francisco L. Urquizo, who handed the Mexican flag to Antonio Cárdenas, reminding him that his men were going to fight with the Allied Nations and that they must represent their country with bravery and honor. Urquizo recalled the moment in his autobiography:

"The ceremonies at Major's Field that today honor all you men of the 201st Squadron give me the opportunity to express the sincere gratitude of my nation and its people towards the Air Force of the United States Army for the training it has offered you. The ties of friendship between our two nations are stronger than ever. Our countries and their people understand that the training of Mexican soldier by the Air Force of the United States Army has created a secure connection that will become stronger still when we

http://www.military.com/HomePage/UnitPageFullText/1,13476,701286,00.html

defeat the Nazis and return peace to humanity."

On behalf of the US, General Barton Young handed the American flag to the Mexicans, which was a highly symbolic and delicate act. The pilots proceeded to board their crafts and deliver a one-hour demonstration of combat techniques, broadcast on television in both countries.

There was a lunch for high-ranking officials of the US army in an office of the Pentagon at which several members of the FAEM were guests. It was there that General Ruben C. Hood, Air Force Chief of State, detailed the training received by the Mexicans and issued a warning regarding the enemy they would be facing: "The Japanese are a sagacious, fanatical and inhuman enemy", which under no circumstances was to be "underestimated, as they neither give nor ask for mercy nor truce" and as such the only response was to reciprocate with "inhumane treatment".

After years of selection, training, uncertainty, penalties and even human loss, the group was finally ready to fight. Or so it seemed. Mere days before embarking, another fatal accident would prevent young graduate Javier Martínez Valle from fulfilling the dream for which he had spent so long preparing. One evening, while following a target released by another aircraft flying at low altitude, Martínez Valle approached at a ninety-degree angle —in a dive, a maneuver for which Mexicans would be famous— collided with the target and lost control of the plane in the late afternoon. His colleagues on the ground realized that his aircraft was behaving strangely and was plummeting towards a swampy area on Padre Island, Texas. It was later deduced that the cable trailed by the aircraft in front had struck the ship of the Mexican pilot.

Dispirited and downhearted, but eager to enter combat against real enemies, the 201st Squadron and the rest of the Mexican Expeditionary Air Force boarded a train headed for the coast of California.

GENERAL URQUIZO HANDS THE MEXICAN FLAG TO
COLONEL CÁRDENAS

Journey to the Far East

On April 8th 1945, the three hundred members of the FAEM
boarded the *Fairisle* in San Francisco Bay, along with 1,500 other
soldiers destined for the Philippines. Colonel Cárdenas Rodríguez
had with him a letter of introduction from the Mexican president
to General Douglas MacArthur, and another for the president of
the Philippines. Prior to their travelling, Lieutenant Colonel
Alfonso Gurza Falfán had flown to the Far East in order to
prepare for the arrival of the FAEM. The month-long crossing
was far from a pleasurable trip. Seasickness and fear of submarine
attacks plagued the crew and kept them in a state of constant
unease, although their celebratory spirits shone through when, at
night, Mexican songs and applause sounded throughout the ship.

In New Guinea, the commander at the US base threw a party
in the Mexicans' honor; they attended a screening of the movie

The Fighting Lady, a documentary about life on board an aircraft carrier. Upon departing the island, the *Fairisle* joined several other boats. "The trip was only tolerable because of the squadron's cheery spirits," wrote one crew member. Sergeant Neftalí González Corona had taken his guitar. "On those stifling nights, you could hear the sound of guitars, the *Canción Mixteca* folk song and other tunes, while the young men played cards sitting around in their lifejackets".[22] Another member of the FAEM, Sergio Carrillo, recalled: "There were 2800 of us soldiers onboard, the vast majority American, all uncertain about our fate; the boat was zigzagging, and the trip took 33 days of anxiety, 33 days of despair." Gallardo remembered: "We mostly travelled at night. They were very cautious in the daytime because of the threat from submarines off the coast of California."

The men of the FAEM could write home, but letters were all subject to censorship. They did not have much to tell, except that during the first week they suffered from severe seasickness which disappeared after some days; that they were vaccinated against malaria and given salt tablets when they began to sweat copiously. They wrote of the sources of entertainment onboard the ship, such as boxing events, and that when they crossed the equator, the crew hosed each other down as per tradition. "There were a lot of days of boredom, too," wrote Enrique Sandoval in his memoirs. "Men dozed in the shade under the gunwale, bridges, hung-out blankets or anything else they could find, even if it meant sitting on the dirty, wet deck." Under the scorching sun, they tried to cool the water in their canteens by throwing them into the sea, tied with a rope, since there was no ice on board. Due to the current, several men lost their canteens in the Pacific Ocean and had to buy others through contraband on the same ship. Fernando Nava Musa, who at 16 had sneaked into the group without being of the required age, had brought a *vitrola* —a device for playing records— and rented it on board for $5 an hour. At the end of the trip, the teenager had $400 in his pocket.

---

[22] Interview with Fernando Nava y Musa, 2014.

When they reached Hollandia on the north coast of New Guinea, the travellers were no longer permitted to escape the heat by sleeping outdoors, due to the risk of airstrikes. Although the area was captured, the boat was heading into dangerous waters. Just before they reached Manila Bay, General Douglas MacArthur telegraphed President Ávila Camacho: "The 201st Squadron is about to join this command. I wish to express to you, Mr. President, the inspiration and pleasure this action arouses…it is personally most gratifying because of my long and intimate friendship with your great people." At the National Palace, Ávila Camacho must have smiled, although the irony surely did not pass him by: MacArthur had played an active part in the US invasion of Veracruz in 1914, and he had even been recommended in the United States to receive the Medal of Honor for bravery.

ARRIVAL IN PHILIPPINES

IV. THE SQUADRON ENTERS COMBAT

"The purpose of regular military personnel is to fight the enemy, to kill or to die. It is not a personal matter. We fought, as part of the Allied Forces, for the ideals of freedom and for the liberation of the world's countries."

Carlos Garduño, 1999

The *Fairisle* docked in Manila Bay on the morning of May 1st 1945. Several hours before, thousands of miles away, Adolf Hitler had swallowed a cyanide capsule and shot himself in the temple upon finding out that the Russians were two blocks away from his bunker. Manila had already been liberated from the Japanese, but Japan had not surrendered yet; although the enemy was in retreat, the archipelago was still in Hirohito's power. The Japanese soldiers had one simple instruction to follow: never to give up. For them, it was victory or death. Close to eighty thousand enemy troops were resisting in the jungle, particularly in the administrative divisions of Luzon and Mindanao. Defeat was unthinkable for Japan: the country had never been successfully invaded, nor had it ever lost a war in all its history. General Kuniaki Koiso, the prime minister, had declared that the final battle was to take place in the Philippines. Earlier that same year, the Japanese had begun to fly on suicide missions, which proved much more effective than conventional warfare. Over seventy

Allied ships had been sunk by the kamikaze attacks; this was the enemy which awaited the 201st Squadron.

The Mexican reinforcements received a warm welcome in Manila, with music and flowers. As Fernando Nava recalled in 2015: "We arrived in the Philippines on May 1st, at around six, and we saw that the bay was full of sunken ships. They told us that we would be disembarking the next morning. I was expecting the enemy to be firing when the gangway came down [to leave the ship]; I thought we would have to run to avoid getting killed. Imagine my surprise, when we got onto the beach, to see an American music band playing, high-ranking officials, and a woman in Puebla dress. I wondered if the boat had brought us to the wrong place: *Where's the war?*, I thought." The woman in traditional Mexican dress, who was photographed kissing the men of the 201st Squadron on the cheek, was Conchita Carmelo, the daughter of the Mexican Honorary Consul in the Philippines.

A war band showed up to play the Mexican national anthem. The men of the FAEM looked at each other in surprise when they heard the joyful notes of the *Zacatecas March* in the warm air of the South Pacific. Apparently the authorities in the Philippines had not been able to get the correct score. The Mexicans said nothing and followed protocol —after all, the *Zacatecas March* was well-known in many parts of the world, and at home it was informally considered as a second national anthem.

The Mexican Honorary Consul was there, too; also General George Kenney, head of air operations at the front, and other officials of the Allied Forces. Kenney wrote about the moment in his autobiography: "After a reception at the pier I took Cardenas over to see General MacArthur, and after the official exchange of greetings, the Mexicans were officially assigned to my command. They then proceeded to Clark Field, where I turned them over to Brigadier General Freddy Smith with instructions to outfit them with P-47s and give them a course of advanced combat training before putting them into action. Both officers and enlisted men were a fine-looking lot and seemed anxious to get to work against the Japs as soon as possible." [23]

The 201st Squadron took a battered train to Florida Blanca, and from there to Clark Field, a base located approximately half a mile north of Manila. The 5th Force had three air squadrons; the Mexicans were the fourth.

On May 2, 1945, at six o'clock in the morning, they raised the Mexican flag with a bamboo stick. Fernando Nava recalled in 2018: "The sun was very bright. Someone took a bamboo to place the flag. Early in the morning we raised Mexico´s flag, the sun was shining, there were some very beautiful clouds, and my record player was playing, that day without a charge, of course. When the flag reached the top of the bamboo, a wind came and it unfolded completely. That moment was very special for us. At that instant we knew that the mission would be carried out with glory."

The Mexican squadron's camp was a muddy clearing in the middle of the jungle, nestled among verdant hills, separate from the Americans' camp. It was rainy season and the tents had dirt floors, so Major Gaxiola Andrade insisted that wooden floors were put into place in order to protect the soldiers from infection and keep their living areas cool. Manuel Cervantes Ramos wrote: "We pitched our tents and built latrines. In the center of the camp, we set up a gazebo with a mast where we could fly our flag every day. It was a few days of hard work, in extremely hot weather with pests and vermin everywhere, since we were surrounded by hills and jungle. We gave street names to the aisles between the tents: 16 de Septiembre, Madero… We also put up a sign saying: '10,000km to the (Mexico City) Zócalo'. It was May 3rd and we would hear shots every now and again, reminding us that it was the Day of the Holy Cross in Mexico —except that what we were hearing were not just harmless fireworks."

Fernando Nava remembered that during the first days they received canned meat, five cigarettes each one, and a roll of toilet paper. Within three days they had built their kitchen and showers,

---

[23] George C. Kenney, General Kenney Reports. *A Personal History of the Pacific War*, Air Force History and Museums Program, 1977, p. 544

and they could take a shower every day. The Mexicans were not overjoyed with the quality of the food at the camp, but conditions improved when several Filipino vendors came to the base to sell them mangos, bananas, beans and other foods to which the Mexicans were more accustomed.

The pilots still had to hold on for several more days while they received an advanced training course for newcomers. A few days before their arrival, Lieutenant Alfonso Garza had come to Luzon to request that the Squadron entered combat immediately, but the request was denied. The Second World War was almost over, and the Mexican pilots were beginning to worry they would not see action. The training program included two days of theory, one of field demonstrations, and various courses: the current situation of the Allied Forces was explained to the men and they were trained in weather-related topics, orienteering, sea rescue techniques, escape and evasion. The practical elements of the program consisted in combat methods, simulated combat missions, and advanced flying techniques.

The uncertainty, demanding conditions, tension regarding what might happen, and quarrelsome nature of the Mexicans combined to cause numerous incidents unfathomable to the Americans. The most serious of these occurred on May 18th, when all hell broke loose between several members of the FAEM at the camp at Porac. Some drunken Mexican soldiers came to blows, and a shot was fired, injuring Corporal Luis Jorge Alfonso López. He had to be hospitalized. The commander of the 201st Squadron, Radamés Gaxiola, was informed of the crimes they had incurred in: false alarm –the gun fight–, insubordination, attempted murder and disobedience. He was asked to impose a sanction and to prevent future recurrence of such incidents, which were disconcerting to the much more disciplined US soldiers. Mexican military law was complex and bureaucratic, requiring an investigation of the events and the formation of military juntas, even for minor transgressions. However, under pressure from the Americans, the Mexicans forewent their procedures and imposed the sanctions there and then.

GENERAL MACARTHUR AND THE PRESIDENT OF THE
PHILIPPINES DISEMBARK IN LEYTE

The beginning of operations helped to defuse the tension. The enemy was retreating, but there were still over two hundred thousand combatants distributed throughout New Guinea, Malaysia, the islands of Palau and Solomon, and, of course, the Philippines. With the exception of Manila, the peninsula of Bataan, Corregidor, and a small area of Luzon, all the Philippine islands were still under Japanese control. At Clark Field, in the middle of the jungle, the Mexicans had their first contact with the reality of the war: at night, they heard detonations from isolated battles between nationalist guerrillas and the enemy. Occasional small parties of Japanese aggressors would appear, or even groups of emaciated prisoners of war liberated by the Allied Forces.

On May 17th, the men finally received the order to board their airplanes. The moment of truth had come.

First mission

The mission of a fighter squadron, one of the most active components in the War of the Pacific, was to escort large marine or air convoys, and utilize their speed and lethal precision to defend ships and larger aircraft in the event that the enemy appeared. The squadrons also constituted the first line of attack on the ground to destroy targets, force the enemy to flee, and clear the way for ground troops. Despite their small size in comparison with units fighting on the ground, the squadrons of thirty pilots were a significant factor in the Pacific War, the last stage of the Second World War. The 201st Squadron had been assigned the P-47s to which they had become accustomed during training. The aircraft had two distinguishing features: its structural strength, which made it less vulnerable to anti-aircraft fire, and, above all, its speed when ascending and manoeuvring, and as such its ability to operate at great altitude. However, its disadvantage came from its weight and size; it was less effective for low-altitude combat and displayed serious limitations under twenty-five thousand feet. The "pecuas" were designed for high altitudes. Although they were reached several times by Japan's anti-aircraft defense, it was rare for one to be brought down. They did, nevertheless, require constant maintenance. According to Urquizo, the P-47s were "a dream for the pilots and a nightmare for the mechanics."

Training missions with old P-47 aircraft, which were in their last hours of service, put the squadron's life at risk. On May 21, Graco Ramírez Garrido's plane broke down in the air and he had to make an emergency landing. The plane was shattered, but the pilot was saved. On May 24, Mario López Portillo was conducting a training flight over Manila Bay when he perceived mechanical damage and tried to return to base. Then his plane's engine exploded. The pilot managed to take his P-47 to the water, parachuted and tried to use his inflatable boat, which did not work either. He was rescued just in time. The members of 201st Squadron were flying on old machines. It is a miracle that there were no more deaths.

The Mexicans received their baptism of fire when they formed a complete detachment wing made up of US fighter planes. Before the men boarded their aircraft, they were all advised to write letters to their families in case they did not survive the mission. The young soldiers embraced each other and boarded their planes. At first, the Squadron did not fly as a single unit, but rather was distributed among other groups of veteran pilots: a common practice for reinforcements, and part of their preparation before being deployed on independent missions.

During one of those joint flights, Reynaldo Gallardo –the pilot who had flown his plane down the main street in Greenville, Texas— performed a spectacular strafing pass against Japanese targets. When he saw the explosions, he pulled his P-47 up into a celebratory roll: a visually impressive display, but one that presented a risk both to the aircraft and to the pilot. One American radio operator was heard to say: "Look at that crazy Mexican." Gallardo was furious, and responded over the radio that he would make him eat his words when he returned to the base. When he stepped down from the aircraft, he saw the pilot he intended to rebuke: a huge man, in comparison with the

Mexican, six feet tall and weighing over two hundred pounds. However, Gallardo's bravado did not waver, despite his being a small man. "He looked at me, bared his teeth in a smile, and asked me if I still wanted to fight. I said, I'll fight you, son of a gun!" However, the situation did not escalate; the pilots were separated and eventually shook hands. Interestingly, rather than dividing the two factions, the incident served as an icebreaker between the Mexicans and the Americans, who found Gallardo's swagger amusing.[24] The quarrel represented the historic nature of its context: two embittered neighbors —one big, one small— joining forces against a mutual enemy. "I never saw a pilot who could fly like Reynaldo Pérez Gallardo", in the words of the legendary pilot Alfonso Cruz Rivera.

In late May, the Squadron was given its first independent mission: to attack a cluster of Japanese troops near to the coast of Luzon. The mission was communicated to the Squadron's leader, Captain Radamés Gaxiola Andrade. The planes took off at eight o'clock in the morning, flying at low altitude over idyllic rainforest landscapes and waterfalls where intense combat was taking place. Their objective was to support the ground troops conquering Philippine territory by bombing enemy bases, buildings, vehicles, artillery and troops. The recon missions were necessary in order to identify targets, although the enemy generally announced their presence by firing at the pilots, who would then attack them. Close to seven thousand US infantry troops of the First Corps guided the Mexican fighter planes. The Japanese were hiding in a forest, firing from caves they would then quickly duck back into. At sundown, the Squadron returned to their base, where their mechanics and armorers refueled their machines and removed their submachine guns to clean them while radio operators checked over the instruments inside the aircraft. The Mexican press, who had a correspondent at Clark Air Base, published the news long-awaited by the Mexican people:

---

[24] Wyllie, John P. "Escuadron 201 Pilot Recalls Mexico's Role in WWII". *La Prensa*, San Diego, California. 9th May 2003.

THE SQUADRON IN CLARK FIELD

"The commander of the 5th American Air Force reports that the Mexican Expeditionary Air Force has entered into combat for the first time against Japanese units. Twenty aircraft from the 201st Squadron under the orders of Captain Radamés Gaxiola took part in the operation, bombing and gunning tanks and trucks in central Luzon. Those who fixed FAEM in their sights as a target were captured the following day by American ground troops. Mexican aviation, acting as a wing of the 58th Combat Group and with their tactical support, received its baptism of fire. The Mexican aircraft were carrying demolition bombs and armed with 50-calibre machine guns. Following the bombing and having destroyed numerous tanks and trucks, they shot at the enemy at very low altitude. The

Japanese responded with anti-aircraft fire, returning the aircraft of Lieutenant Carlos Garduño Díaz with two blows to the wings."

Mexico's first casualty of the war came during their mission of June 1st, the most noteworthy of all their missions. It was a dangerous mission: to destroy a Japanese ammunition depot near Vigan, on the eastern coast of Luzon. In addition to anti-aircraft fire, the unit had three natural surrounding defenses in the form of high cliffs; the only possible approach was from the sea and through a narrow opening. Major Gaxiola suggested that the only way to destroy the depot was to dive bomb it from a very high altitude – virtually a suicide mission, given the weight of the P-47s. The Americans said it could not be done, but Gaxiola Andrade assured them that the Aztec Eagles could. He requested that Carlos Garduño volunteered.[25]

Four aircraft, flown by Carlos Garduño Núñez, Fausto Vega, Miguel Moreno Arreola and Praxedis López Ramos, launched themselves at the target. "That was our first mission involving dive bombing," explained Garduño years later. "The high command authorized it when they found out the Mexican squadron contained dive bombing experts. Fausto [Vega Santander] was coming up behind me, right on my tail. First I dropped my bombs and I got out straight away, grazing the sea. My blackout happened and when I got my vision back, my plane was ascending, I turned around to see if Fausto was behind me... but it was another plane; the leader of the second unit was following me and signaling to me with his mic in hand. I connected my mic and heard: 'They took Cachito out!'" Opinions vary as to what caused the incident; many reject the notion that it was a Japanese projectile, although according to the testimony of

---

[25] This information is corroborated by American sources who claim that the US Navy and Air Force had unsuccessfully attacked the site before General George Kenney was informed that the Mexican Air Force had pilots trained in dive bombing. See George C. Marshall, Foundation & Virginia Military Institute, *The Journal of Military History*. Volume 66, Issues 3-4, 2002.

at least two Mexican pilots and eyewitnesses, Vega was in fact brought down by enemy fire. According to the Official History of the FAEM, Vega Santander simply lost control of his plane: "The accident was caused by descending too steeply; when he tried to bring the plane out of the dive, it went into what is known in aerodynamics as a high-speed stall, causing the aircraft to lurch twice to the right, losing considerable altitude and hitting the water at around three fifty miles an hour and instantly bursting into flames." [26]

What really happened? In 1945, Garduño wrote in his logbook: "We found the target at ten minutes past eleven – we released the bombs and began diving at around eleven fifteen. I was already descending and counting: one thousand and one, two thousand and one... up to five thousand. I pulled the trigger on my machine guns, hoping to dodge the enemy fire, and on the count of five I dropped my bombs and came out of the dive at maximum air velocity. I had to pull the lever hard and everything went black. I went up to six thousand five hundred rapidly, and I saw the target covered in black smoke...a white spot near the beach caught my eye. It was Cacho's plane that had gone into the water."[27] "They hit his plane near the cabin," according to Miguel Moreno Arreola. "I thought I saw something coming away from the damaged P-47, which then reeled to the right and hit the water. Garduño ticked me off because I abandoned the formation to fly over the crash site, while the Japanese were still shooting at me. I just saw my comrade's lifejacket floating adrift." Moreno's own testimony stated: "I realized that the aircraft in front of me, which was being flown by Fausto Vega Santander, was spinning

---

[26] Sandoval Castarrica, Enrique. *Historia Oficial de la Fuerza Aérea Expedicionaria Mexicana*, pp. 318. Defence Ministry, 1946.

[27] In 1999 Garduño referred to Vega Santander as the only casualty that occurred during combat. In 1993 detailed this mission accurately in an interview with the Institute of Oral History, at the University of Texas, where he called it the most important mission of the 201st Squaron. See: Interview with Carlos Garduño by Alicia de Jong-Davis, 1993, "Interview no. 891," Institute of Oral History, University of Texas at El Paso.

(…) straight after trying to exit the dive. The next thing I saw was the plane hitting the water upside down and exploding." Search and rescue workers never found the soldier's body. *El Nacional* reported that Vega's death was a "huge wake-up call that we need to remember at all times that we are at war." Ávila Camacho's government even compared the loss of the pilot to the sacrifice of the Boy Soldiers of Chapultepec, six Mexican teenage cadets who died defending Mexico from US forces in 1847, and he reminded the public that the 201st Squadron was fighting "for Mexico's honor and dignity".

Two days later, pilot José Espinosa Fuentes nobly sacrificed himself while trying to take off in a newly-repaired aircraft, despite the fact that he was not obligated to check the mechanical state of the equipment. Some reports state that he had volunteered.[28] The P-47 lost power immediately after takeoff, near the town of Florida Blanca, Luzon. Procedure in the event of such an occurrence was that the aircraft should attempt an emergency landing at the end of the runway. However, US soldiers had pitched their tents in that area, so Espinosa elected to turn right and collide with a sugar mill. His aircraft caught fire and he burned to death. He was twenty-six years old, and had married less than a year earlier, in Mazatlán.

His loss was felt deeply in the camp. Colonel Ed Roddy, commander of the 58th Combat Group, approached Captain Andrade to ask if he wanted to lower the Mexican flag at half-mast. The captain, however, replied that no man was above the Republic and as such the flag should be flown at full-mast. Moved, Roddy responded: "201 is part of the team. We will lower our flag to half-staff to honor our fallen comrade". He promptly ordered the American flag to be flown at half-mast. The gesture impressed the Mexicans and helped to increase mutual respect with the Americans. As the days went by, the Mexicans gradually earned the Americans' trust.

---

[28] *Low Rider Magazine*, volume 22, pp 20. Park Avenue Design, 2002.

THE SQUADRON WITH A BOMB DEDICATED TO
HIROHITO, WITH LOVE: "TRIP TO TOKYO WITH TEQUILA".

But the American and Australian troops in the Philippines also resented the Mexicans´ poor discipline and what they saw as favoritism and a soft-hand attitude towards their Latin American comrades. Turmoil was common in the Aztec camp, there were plenty of high-speed infractions, arrests for disorder — especially the use of alcoholic beverages—, fights "and the occasional abuse in neighboring towns". Although the reports don´t mention which abuses, there was most probably assistance to brothels and deals with prostitutes. On one occasion there were shots in the heat of a party, an unimaginable offense for soldiers of other nationalities.

In the first month alone in the Philippines, there were 28 arrests for misconduct, one per day, or 10% of the entire Mexican expeditionary force. "The military and internal discipline of 201st Squadron", wrote Enrique Sandoval Castarrica in his official history, "cannot be considered completely satisfactory (...) It was strange to the North American command that our faults would not be punished with the same energy that their regulations impose." As it had been determined that police offenses would be resolved by the Mexican command itself, and in many cases they depended on judges working in Mexico City, sanctions were impossible. The Mexican command saw as normal many situations that were cause for horror for the American troops. However, the mutual sympathy never died out and the Americans ended up getting used to the quarrelsome and somewhat carefree nature of the Mexicans.

SHORTLY BEFORE TAKING OFF

"The Americans would call us white noses", Reynaldo Pérez Gallardo recalled years later in an interview on his eightieth birthday. "They called us that because our mechanics had painted the noses of our planes in white. We became very popular. On one occasion I was at the hospital, being treated for some minor issues, when a wounded soldier next to me realized I wasn't American. He was in a bad way, but he got up and came over to my bed. He asked me, "Do you fly a white nose?', and I told him I did. He hugged me and said, 'You have no idea how much we love you guys.'"

Glorious eagles

In June, the US troops intensified their march through the jungle and the most ruthless phase of the fighting began. The backdrop to the battle against the troops of General Tomoyuka Yamashita moved from the rice paddies to the mountains; such a delicate situation meant backup from the air was vital, although the targets were becoming harder to locate as the action moved deeper within the jungle and the enemy all but disappeared into the foliage. Frequent storms made flying difficult; when the weather was rough, a recon aircraft would first fly low over where the Japanese troops were, marking out the area with purple-colored smoke and then radioing Gaxiola Andrade to confirm that his men could proceed.

The planes of the 201st Squadron would approach the area one by one, diving down in the face of enemy fire, dropping their bombs and then ascending again, just in time to avoid being hit by the flying debris and battling the enormous gravitational pressure that could cause pilots to faint. "We got it into our heads that we were going to show the Americans what we could do; what we were made of," recalled pilot Reynaldo Gallardo, years later. "Get near the target, make sure I hit it —and hit it good, to cause as much damage as I could— then quickly turn around and get out of there. [The Americans asked me:] 'Hey, who's that guy doing circles over the target?' 'It's Pancho Pistolas!' I laughed."

On June 14th, a US platoon from Group 58 of the fighter commando guided the Squadron to fire at Japanese positions by the Marikina Dam, east of Manila. Also around mid-June, Héctor Espinosa Galván spotted an enemy detachment on a back road two and a half miles from Payawan. The lieutenant ordered his squad of seven aircraft to attack immediately: "We approached the target directly, firing our machine guns. I took aim at a truck that was right in front of me, we went closer and I fired off two bursts; the vehicle went up in flames almost straight away. We ascended rapidly to avoid the explosions once we had dropped our bombs. The enemy responded forcefully with small arms, damaging two of our planes." On June 20, Japanese anti-aircraft fire hit Pratt Ramos's plane, who remained in the air and survived. June 26th saw the Squadron bomb isolated troops in Infanta in the province of Quezon. By then, there were still over twenty-three thousand Japanese men on the mountain.

On June 28th, the 201st Squadron saw their most dangerous fight. Divided into two groups of twelve fighters, the Mexicans dropped twenty-three tons of explosives over twenty-four flights of attack on the enemy, who was resisting to the east of Luzon. In early July, the Allies began their frontal attack on Japanese territory. The 201st Squadron was assigned a mission even riskier than previous ones: to go ahead of the US navy and sweep the stretch of sea going from Manila to Okinawa, passing over the island of Formosa (modern-day Taiwan), a dangerous stronghold of the Japanese. These fighter sweeps, also called "Rhubarb missions", were aimed at locating and containing, destroying or damaging air defenses in the South China Sea. The distances involved would test the pilots and aircraft to their limits; the planes barely carried enough fuel for the return flights. Any diversion, miscalculation or unforeseen weather could mean death, and that was without taking into account the potential for anti-aircraft fire.

On July 6th the planes left Clark Air Base, weighed down with bombs, and headed north, the inclement sun heating the insides of their cabins to almost intolerable temperatures. The Squadron did not find any obstacles on Formosa. They advanced through the skies until they had completed their mission, barely making it back to Clark Air Base —except for Lieutenant Pérez, who was forced to land in Lingayen, one hundred and twenty miles north, due to a fuel shortage. "In early July," wrote James P. Gallagher in his memoirs, "one plane from the Mexican squadron with fuel problems paid our strip a visit after a fighter sweep over Formosa. While the Mexican insignia was used on some of the P-47s, this one retained US markings. Its rudder, however, sported the red, white and green of the Mexican flag. I spent an hour or so chatting in simple English with the pilot, Reynaldo Pérez Gallardo. When he taxied away for takeoff, heading on to Clark Field, I threw him a salute... and he tossed me a thumbs-up". [29] The pilots were so drained upon their return that they needed help disembarking from their aircraft.

Tragedy struck the Aztec Eagles once again on July 16th. The group was flying from the Philippines to New Guinea in the middle of a storm, when, around thirty miles off the island of Biak, Captain Espinosa Galván —who was considered one of the best pilots of the group— reported that he had suffered a fuel leak and that he would attempt a water landing. His comrades looked on in horror as his aircraft sank like a stone, with no trace of its pilot appearing. The formation had to continue on to Biak, whence Lieutenant Roberts left to search in vain for the captain. The loss of Espinosa, a flight leader, was a hard blow for the team. Despite the fact that more Mexicans were currently being trained in the US in case the war was prolonged, for the time being, the Eagles had lost a substantial portion of their operative capacity.

Three days later, the group lost sight of Captain Pablo Rivas Martínez and Lieutenant Guillermo García Ramos while flying through a storm from Biak back to the Philippines. Both men were on a mission that absorbed the time of the Aztec Eagles for weeks: transporting new planes from Biak, New Guinea, to the outskirts of Manila. It was a journey of 2,300 kilometers, equivalent to the distance between Mexico City and San Diego, in a tiny cabin, with barely enough fuel, and with temperatures of more than 45 degrees.

---

[29] James P. Gallagher, *With the Fifth Army Air Force*, Johns Hopkins University Press, p. 124.

The storm took them by surprise. High wind speeds caused García's cabin to detach from his aircraft mid-flight. "We flew directly into the storm, using our instruments. I had a short conversation on the radio with the captain: `It seems to me that it would be better to go up, because if something abnormal happens to us in these conditions, we could not do anything other than to parachute´"´, as he detailed in his official report. "The storm became more intense, with heavy rains, powerful electrical discharges and very strong convection currents. The captain (Pablo Rivas) veered to the right, ascending." García tried to communicate with Rivas, but the lightnings damaged his radio.

GUILLERMO GARCÍA READY FOR TAKE OFF

Blindly, the pilot flew through the instruments of his aircraft; he found an island, looked for a place to land, but saw that it was impossible. He then decided to use his parachute and fell into the sea, a short distance from an island in New Guinea that had been seized by the Japanese. General Urquizo's memoirs claim that

García landed in the water and sailed to shore on an inflatable raft. Actually, he struggled to stay afloat all night, and it was not until dawn that he was able to enable his boat. García then reached a small beach. Throughout the rest of the day, he struggled to remain hidden, and spent the night on his raft. He heard a bomber pass above but could not signal it because it was too dark. The greatest danger he faced other than capture by the Japanese was the enormous boas native to the island.

In the morning, he spotted an aircraft formation overhead and sent them signals using a mirror. Captain Larry Dennis Osborne saw the reflections and alerted the other pilots. Despite fears it could be a trap, a Catalina rescue seaplane descended to the island amid violent waves and successfully retrieved Guillermo García.

The Mexican press received news of the rescue in late August of that year, electing to add the colorful detail that at some point, the pilot had had to defend himself from an "angry-looking boar". The other pilot, Pablo Rivas Martínez, was never found. In the hopes that he might one day appear, shipwrecked on an island, the Mexican government did not declare him dead until 1947, and his family waited many more years after that, despite rumors that Rivas Martínez had survived as a "cripple" and decided to stay in the Philippines.[30] The final casualty was Lieutenant Mario López Portillo, who lost control of his plane on July 21st in the middle of a summer storm, crashing into a mountain near Luzon. Twenty-three years old, he had been one of the team's most capable and responsible pilots and had an impeccable service record.

Many years later, the mechanic Luis Guzmán recalled the painful search for the body of López Portillo. In the torrid climate on the mountain, they emptied their canteens and ran out of water. Near a slope, they heard a murmur that sounded like a stream. They followed the noise, hoping to find water, but to their horror they saw that the sound was made by clouds of insects and ants that were devouring the corpse of their fallen companion.

---

[30] Author interview with Alma Rosa Rivas-Castaño, granddaughter of the pilot.

Back in Mexico, the US ambassador informed his country that the Mexican public were taking the news of the men's deaths very well, almost stoically, "somewhat fatalistic", and even proudly. He reported that there was "an acceptance of losses comparable with a people who have long been engaged in an extended war," and that the Mexicans showed "obvious pride in the fact that Mexican blood had been shed as proof of their participation as an Allied Nation of a victorious and powerful coalition". The Aztec Eagles displayed great talent once again on August 8th during one of their last bombing missions over Karenko, Formosa (Taiwan), led by Colonel Amadeo Castro Almaza. The planes had to fly so low they almost touched the water in order to stay off Japanese radar, but what made the mission even more difficult was the fact that each aircraft was carrying a bomb weighing nearly half a ton on its right wing and a near-empty fuel tank on its left. When they dropped the first bomb on a group of buildings in the port of Karenko, Lieutenant Castro lost control of his aircraft due to the sudden imbalance. He began to spiral, but managed to regain control in time to warn his comrades of what would happen when they dropped their bombs. Having completed their mission successfully, the Eagles separated in order to refuel at different landing sites.

News reaches home

Back in Mexico, the press was eagerly lapping up the adventures of the 201st Squadron, reporting on them as soon as news reached their offices; but they tended not to be aware of the details. There were a few correspondents at Clark Field and in Porac who sent news back to their papers. This meant the press was reporting on the Squadron's baptism of fire before the Ministry of Defense could do so, which displeased the governmental body. In general, the newspapers never missed a chance to report on the men's supposedly glorious escapades in the exaggerated style typical of the era; even going so far as to invent stories based on unconfirmed scraps of information which at times verged on the fanciful. On June 13th, *El Universal* reported in an eight-page spread a clearly apocryphal statement from the head of Pacific operations: "The 201st Squadron is being covered with glory, declares General MacArthur". "It was an unforgettable deed," said *El Nacional* of the group's first mission; and a few days later, "The Mexican flag conquers gloriously on the Philippine front". This gave the impression that the thirty brave pilots were defeating the Empire of the Rising Sun by themselves, and the papers lamented the losses of their men as if they were on the same scale as those on the Russian front.

Close to the end of the war, *El Popular* reported that Cantinflas, the famous comedian, was travelling out to cheer on the members of the Squadron. The printed press loved to write about the men they had dubbed the "eaglets", boasting about the supposed "great spirits at the Mexican camp," ignoring the tragedies occurring while trivializing the soldiers' missions with the impression that Clark Air Base was virtually a picnic in the jungle, with Mexican folk songs, flowers and dances. They also announced the upcoming production of a Hollywood movie about the group's exploits. On a more critical note, the paper *Novedades* reported that Antonio Cárdenas, commander of the FAEM, earned more money than Mexico's Secretary of Defense, Lázaro Cárdenas (no relation), which may have led Francisco Urquizo to declare that only the Ministry of Defense could report on the activities of the FAEM in order to avoid the spread of rumors and false alarms.

Petitions sprang up in various towns around Mexico to name schools after the Squadron, and governors of several states – notably Jalisco, where many of the pilots had roots– saw the chance to increase their political capital by setting up tributes to the men and delivering passionately patriotic speeches, despite the fact the soldiers had not yet returned from the Philippines. Ávila Camacho and Cárdenas elected to wait until the war was over. It is not known if they were harboring territorial ambitions –perhaps a latent desire to re-establish some jurisdiction over the Philippines, where the Mexican pilots were more popular than the

Americans– but in any case, if they were hoping to gain greater influence in the archipelago, the 1946 formation of the Third Republic in Manila put such hopes to rest.

Return to America

The final act of the War of the Pacific began with the invasion of Okinawa, involving fierce air combat between allied fighters and Japanese suicide pilots. The 201st Squadron, lacking in operative capacity due to the death of its command pilots, did not participate in the invasion. In a letter dated July 24th, Captain Radamés Gaxiola told the government that "in light of the regrettable losses the Squadron has suffered over the course of its operations, and due to the fact that to date no replacements have been received, I make it known to my superiors that with the loss of those who occupied positions of command in the air team, that said team has been debilitated since the remaining personnel *lack experience in leading formations in combat.*

Considering that the potential move north would involve much more intense operations, I am of the opinion that the move north should be delayed until, by means of combat operations from this place, new elements for positions of command can be created." Gaxiola's communiqué confirmed what US officials had already decided: that the fallen Mexicans had been the most capable and essential pilots, and without them the group was debilitated and had no offensive capacity. High-ranking US officials considered that the percentage of casualties in relation to the number of pilots was very high. [31] Naturally, the decision to withdraw the Mexican soldiers from combat had not been down to Gaxiola, but General MacArthur. Mexican replacements were already being trained up in the States, but the surrender of the Japanese Empire following Hiroshima and Nagasaki eliminated any possibility of sending a new generation of pilots to the fighting front.

---

[31] Schwab, p. 1135

P-47 PLANE WITH MEXICAN INSIGNIA

One night in late August, while the Mexicans were watching a movie at the Clark camp, Captain Radamés Gaxiola appeared in an agitated state. The projection was stopped and all the men stood to attention, wary of the possibility that an attack was occurring or an emergency mission was imminent. Gaxiola informed them that the encampment of the 5th Force had received a message: the US had dropped an extremely powerful bomb on Japan; one so destructive that Hirohito had surrendered unconditionally. With no clear grasp yet of the magnitude of what had occurred, the members of the Squadron cheered and whooped, although they may have been somewhat disappointed that they had not been in Okinawa to witness the capitulation.

The intrepid team would still have to fulfill one final mission before going home. In late August, the Mexicans escorted a convoy of ships travelling to Okinawa in Japan. The war was over, but there were still Japanese kamikaze units dotted around the Pacific who would rather die than surrender and were lying in wait for the Allies in order to inflict as much damage as possible. The 201st Squadron´s task was to head them off if they appeared. Until that point, the "eaglets", as they were known in Mexico, had not entered combat against other fighter planes. That day, they were prepared. For twelve tense hours on August 26th 1945, the Aztec Eagles flew overhead the ships, detecting two planes that quickly disappeared into the clouds. When they reached Formosa, where there was a Japanese stronghold, stress levels peaked; fortunately, the mission came to an end uneventfully.

In October of that year, Japan withdrew from the island of Formosa, but for years and even decades, many Japanese continued to carry out their duties on some of the more than seven thousand islands that make up the Philippines. In the final days a small group of land staff from the FAEM became involved in a related incident. On August 26th, the day of the Squadron's final mission, Lieutenant José Cruz Abundis left Clark Field with a group of ten troops in pursuit of a mission, and was ambushed by eight Japanese soldiers. The men reacted by drawing their weapons, and then realized that another enemy was moving in the opposite direction, ready to throw hand grenades at them. According to Abundis' report, shots were fired, resulting in the capture of two Japanese and no Mexican casualties.

When the war finished, over fifty thousand Japanese soldiers who had formed part of the group known as Shobu descended the mountain. However, not all of them had grasped the fact that the hostilities were over. The last Japanese soldier to surrender was Hiroo Onoda in 1974, having been hidden in the mountains on the archipelago for nearly thirty years. When the time came for the men to return home, the Philippine authorities paid grateful tribute to the Allied forces, with particular attention to the FAEM: ostensibly because they were the only ones who understood Spanish, but also for their modest but irreproachable participation despite the soldiers' lack of experience and the fact that, as a country, they had made an exception and choosing for the first time to become involved in an international war. In the eyes of the Filipino people, all of this made the eaglets' contribution even more valuable. On September 16th –Mexican Independence Day– General Basilio J. Valdez, Secretary of Defense of the Philippines, inspected the Mexican troops at Clark Field, presented six of the men with the Philippine Liberation Medal and hoisted the Mexican flag while a P-47 roared overhead.

A fair assessment

To what extent did the 201st Squadron contribute to the victory in the War of the Pacific? In Mexico the achievements of the team were somewhat exaggerated and there was a shortage of truly impartial assessments, in part because they were not really necessary. Some non-flying members of the FAEM, such as cooks, mechanics and medics, eager for their share of the glory, told highly implausible feats that the Mexican press reported as gospel with no attempt at probing further into their truthfulness. For example, one mechanic claimed, in an interview with Mario Escurida from *Así* magazine, that he and a group of five men had fought hordes of Japanese soldiers in the jungle, taking prisoners and confiscating Japanese flags, which they then flew at the US base.[32] Many others tended to exaggerate and embellish their stories, remembering Clark Field as a Mexican picnic and the members of the Squadron as a happy gang. The truth is some of them came back with post-battle stress and suffered from nightmares and night terrors.[33]

The embellishments were harmless enough, but a fair assessment is one that strikes a balance between the grandiose and triumphant official narrative of the time, the tendency of the veterans in years to come to misrepresent their actions during the war, and the lack of recognition –bordering on disdain– coming from American sources of information. As ever, the truth lies somewhere in between. Viewed objectively, it must be acknowledged that the actions of the Mexican Expeditionary Force were valiant, determined and honorable; however, as historian Stephen Schwab explained, they also came too late and were limited and largely symbolic.

When the FAEM arrived in the Far East, the battle over the Philippines had virtually been won by the Americans. The Squadron's duty consisted of eliminating the last remaining

---

[32] El Escuadrón 201. *Así* magazine, issue 261, 1st December 1945.

[33] Author interview with José Luis Barbosa Cerda, April 2019.

strongholds with the help of the US Air Force. There were many fatalities –five Mexican pilots lost their lives over the Pacific in just one month– and the number of non-combat accidents was unusually high. In their defense, the training that the Mexicans received had been rushed, and the Squadron had been dispatched to a fighting front on which their American fellow fighters had years of experience. The language barrier may have also contributed to some of the casualties. However, no member of the Squadron, either during or after, ever complained about the disadvantage at which they found themselves when they were sent to the Far East. They spoke of those days as a simple fulfillment of their duty as soldiers. Several features of the P-47 planes also limited the Squadron's potential. The planes had a low fuel capacity and therefore struggled to fly long distances, particularly while carrying explosives. Generally speaking, the Mexican pilots were operating under very challenging conditions.

The group took part in a total of fifty-three missions in the Philippines and four on Formosa, which involved greater flying distances, in addition to numerous ship escort missions, all within a period of just over thirty days.[34] The majority of these missions were planned, but some were emergencies. In all, forty-five were successful, with a high percentage of hits when bombing land targets. The 201st Squadron never fought Japanese aircraft directly, since enemy pilots concentrated in their own country in order to defend the territory. This meant that the Mexicans did not bring down any Japanese planes. In terms of individual takeoffs, the Aztec Eagles accumulated 785 defensive missions with an average of eighty-two hours per pilot, and six offensive missions, reaching a total of two thousand hours of combat in the Philippines and on Formosa –much more than the American squadrons over the same time period. The squad dropped a total

---

[34] Vega Rivera, José G. *The Mexican Expeditionary Air Force in World War II: The Organization, Training, and Operations of the 201st Squadron.* A Research Paper Presented To The Research Department Air Command and Staff College In Partial Fulfillment of the Graduation Requirements of ACSC, 1997.

of 1,457 bombs on occupied territory, and it is calculated that they eliminated, nullified or expelled around thirty thousand Japanese soldiers,[35] as well as destroying vital enemy infrastructures, weaponry and convoys of supplies or reinforcements. They lost just one aircraft in combat, and almost all their missions were successfully accomplished. US Air Force reports indicate that Mexican bombing and machine gun missions were carried out to a satisfactory standard. They also committed heroic acts, such as that of Fausto Vega Santander, who died annihilating the Japanese bastion on Vigan with his venturesome diving pass.[36] However, in a confidential report undertaken following Japan's surrender, General Kenney was critical and recommended that the Squadron returned home as soon as possible.

"To date six (*sic*) pilots have been lost and fourteen aircraft have been wrecked. One pilot has been grounded and two are recovering from injuries incurred in accidents; one of these may eventually be permanently grounded. As a result of this attrition the effective strength of this unit has been reduced to twenty-three active pilots. Of the remaining pilots there are two who can be called satisfactory leaders, a fact which in itself has probably been the most important

---

[35] Statistic provided by Henry H. Arnold, commander of the US Armed Forces at the ceremony in Mexico City's Military Casino in August 1944. See Enrique Sandoval Castarrica, *op cit* pp. 413. Likely not an accurate statistic. Arnold was probably referring to a number to which the Squadron *contributed*.

[36] Especially author Santiago A. Flores has defended the theory that Fausto Vega Santander died during a training mission, not in action of war. However, the evidence presented by him has not been conclusive, since it relies more on the absence of mentions of the incident in the memoirs of some military officers, Vega´s death certificate —written one year later—, as well as the existence of an alleged journal written *in situ* by Fernando Hernández Vega, a member of the Squadron, that he has not produced so far. Contrary to his affirmation, is the testimony of Carlos Garduño, in command of that mission and an eyewitness, who described it in high detail during an interview with Alicia Jong-Davis in 1993; as well as the testimony of Maximiliano Gutiérrez Marín, ground staff, who knew other eye witnesses: "Since I remember, Carlos Garduño, Miguel Moreno and Praxedis López Ramos always affirmed that *Cacho* was killed in combat". Major Dennis A. Cavagnaro supports these testomonies.

cause for the marked decline in the efficiency of this organization." [37]

It is not clear whether Kenney was expressing dissatisfaction regarding the performance of the Squadron or was merely concerned about further loss of life. Military historians consider the War of the Pacific to have been one of the most dangerous, demanding and deadly battles in World War II. Although the 201st Squadron contributed with undeniable bravery, particularly at the Battle of Luzon, their odyssey was a drop in the ocean in terms of the war as a whole. In comparison with the nearly two million US and Filipino troops, or the war's twenty-seven million Russian casualties, the thirty Mexican pilots and their five lost souls are barely a footnote in the pages of history. The Mexican propaganda machine exaggerated the team's importance, while its American counterpart treated them as a mere afterthought. But for those thirty pilots it was irrelevant how many Mexicans had been dispatched to the Pacific: for them, the war was as merciless, perilous and real as for any Russian, British or German soldier. A balanced assessment was prepared by Far East Air Force, the military aviation organization of the US Army in the Philippines:

> "In view of the fact that the squadron represented picked men, perhaps a higher level might have been expected. On the other hand, considering the language barrier and the relatively short operational training experience, their record is nothing to apologize for, particularly when it is remembered that the ground support techniques used by the Fifth Fighter Command on Luzon were the development of two long years of experience and had reached a height of efficiency and effectiveness."

While it is true that the battle in the Pacific was already won before the Mexicans arrived, that was not their true motive for

---

[37] Kenney, letter to Commander General, 3. Quoted in Schwab, p. 1136.

going. Mexico risked more than was necessary not merely to cooperate with a cause that many citizens supported –liberating the people of the Philippines, with whom Mexico shared a three-hundred-year history– but also to earn itself a place in the United Nations, and particularly to reestablish its relationship with the US on more equitative grounds, which it effectively accomplished. Without a doubt, the 201st Squadron's most important victory consisted of flying Mexico towards the post-war world; it is for this honorable sacrifice that they deserve all the glory.

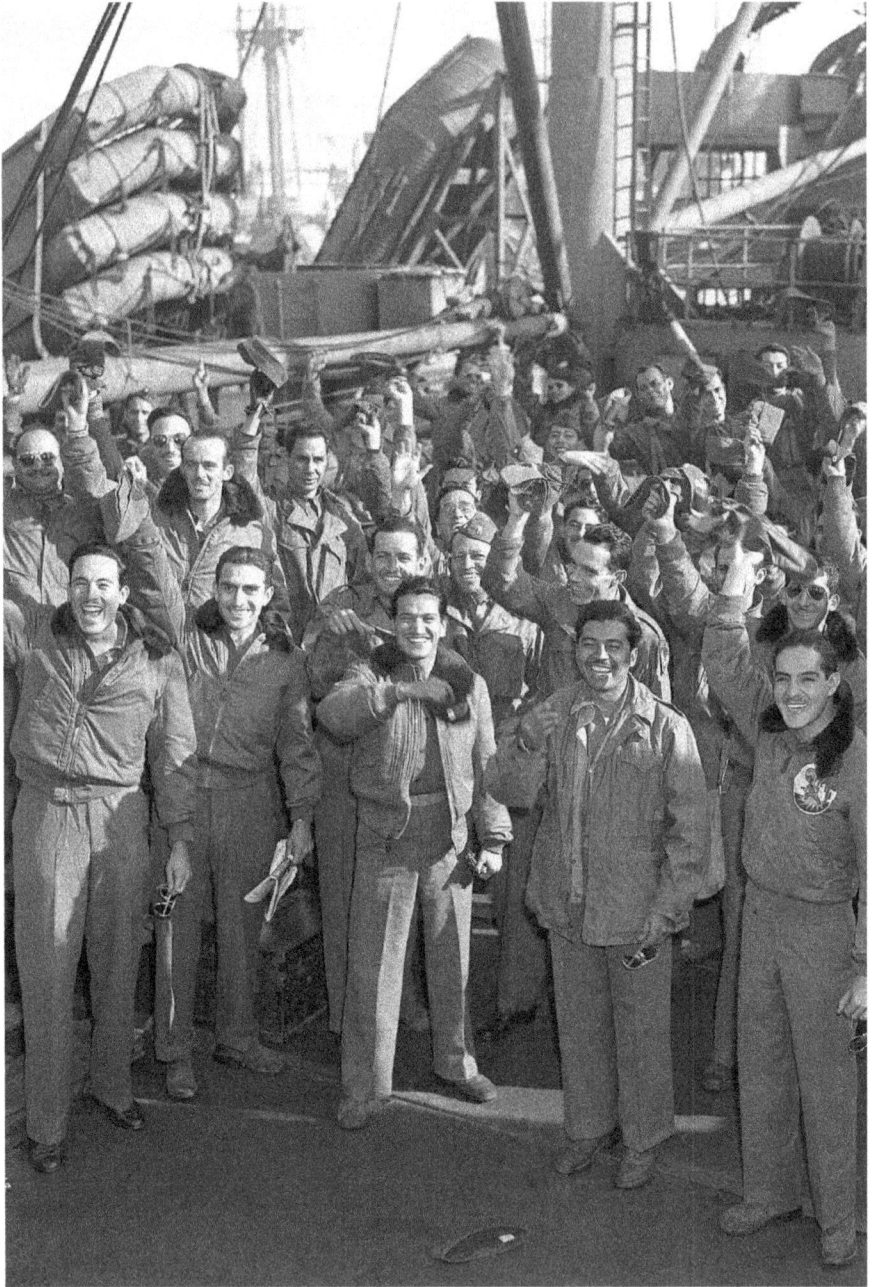

ARRIVAL IN LOS ANGELES ON NOV. 13, 1945

V. RETURN HOME AND LEGACY

"The Mexican Air Force, which has been an honor for me
to include in this Command, has performed admirably.
Their commanders proved to be true comrades in arms".

Letter from Douglas MacArthur to Ávila Camacho, August 19th 1945

The Squadron set foot back in Mexico City at Buenavista Station: the same place from which they had departed. They had been travelling by boat for ten days since leaving Manila on October 23rd, their spirits high and with none of the anxiety that had plagued them previously that they might run into German submarines along the way, although the absence of their fallen brothers was palpable. Some had burned or drowned to death, and at least one had been lost to the immense Pacific. In stark contrast to their arrival in the US in 1944, which had been quiet and distrustful, their return through Los Angeles on November 13th 1945 was celebrated with embraces, confetti and flowers from the Latino community and even some Americans.

Over thirty thousand people, mainly Mexican residents of the city, filled the streets holding up a sign proclaiming "Welcome home". From there, they took a train back along the same route by which they had arrived: they marched through Nuevo Laredo waving the Mexican flag while twenty-one farewell salvos were fired by the Americans at Fort McIntosh.

It was in Nuevo Laredo that, "with tanned faces, bright yellow from the Atabrine and sporting American green steel helmets, khaki shirts and pants, and army boots, with a small backpack on their backs and a lightweight M-1 over their shoulders", the FAEM set foot back on national territory. There, a small act of protocol took place between the authorities of the two countries. They stopped off in Monterrey, Saltillo, San Luis Potosí —where they ate their first traditional meal, *mole de guajolote* and tortillas— and Querétaro, where the train stopped so that people could gift the men flowers along with applause, kisses, and smiles, immortalized in historical photographs.

On November 18th 1945, they received a heroes' welcome in Mexico City. When the train pulled in, hundreds of people were waiting there to see their returning soldiers. The first man to step down onto the platform was Captain Antonio Cárdenas, who was quickly handed a microphone. He could not conceal his emotion. "Beloved people of Mexico," he called out, his voice cracking, "on behalf of the Expeditionary Troops, I send you our greatest and most impassioned greeting. I am grateful for your display of kindness and affection." A convoy then transported the members of the Squadron down Madero Avenue, passing beneath countless triumphal arches as people cheered them on until they reached the town square. It was the first time such a large number of people had gathered there spontaneously: the Squadron was paraded "in the brilliant sunshine as confetti fell from the balconies and terraces onto the heads of the Eaglets, and a crowd of people in their finest clothes applauded enthusiastically until they were hoarse from whooping," as the newspaper Excélsior described the scene.

"Coming back to Mexico was amazing. I was nominated to carry the flag, but it was a huge thing and I could not lift it up. I cried like a baby that day," recalled Miguel Moreno Arreola. In the various interviews given by members of the FAEM, they stated that while in the Philippines, they had believed they would never see their homeland again, and much less a tribute such as the one that greeted them. At one point, while they were travelling down Juárez Avenue in Mexico City, the fiancée of one of the members jumped into the passing parade and into her lover's arms. "[People] came over and tore strips off our clothing to keep as a souvenir of us heroes," remembered Sergio Carrillo of the FAEM, years later. In the town square, the Squadron greeted President Ávila Camacho again, along with the Secretary of the Treasury of the United States Henry Margenthau and Amalia Solórzano, Lázaro Cárdenas's wife. General Antonio Cárdenas handed the president the Mexican flag. "You all have returned in glory," declared Ávila, "having fulfilled your duty with excellence, and now, in this historic plaza, the people thank you. Generals, chiefs, officials and troops of the Expeditionary Air Force, I receive with emotion the flag which the country has entrusted you." There was a widespread sense of relief: the biggest, bloodiest and most expensive war in the history of the world had come to an end. Faced with the uncertainty of a post-war world, Mexico was certain about one thing: it had taken part, just in time to win, and lost just five men.

The monument in Chapultepec

Two weeks later, a movie named *El Escuadrón 201* starring Sarah García and Domingo Soler was released in theatres all over the country. President Ávila promised to erect a large monument in the historic forest of Chapultepec –but when construction finally finished, Mexico had another president, and the world had moved on. An arguably more worthy monument was the school that pilot Ángel Bocanegra requested of the president in 1944, before going to war. To this day, the school is still standing in Tepoztlán, Morelos. It was there, in the building suggested by the young soldier, that members of the FAEM continued to meet for many years after the war was over.

During a visit from General Henry H. Arnold, commander in chief of the Allied Air Forces, in October 1945, he stated that "the pilots of the Mexican Expeditionary Air Force used their machine guns, fragmentation and fire bombs, against enemy columns, against the artillery and against tanks and trucks. We must acknowledge them the merit of putting thirty thousand Japanese out of combat."

General Douglas MacArthur wrote in a letter to Ávila Camacho dated October 27th that he would recommend Colonel Cárdenas Rodríguez and Captain Radamés Gaxiola for the Legion of Merit decoration, which had been created by Franklin D. Roosevelt in 1942. Colonel Antonio Cárdenas Rodríguez went on to receive the medal from Harry S. Truman for demonstrating "exceptional leadership abilities over his units in combat operations against the Japanese, supervising and participating in numerous attacks on enemy-controlled positions. He conducted his forces in successful attacks, effectively destroying enemy ships, facilities and men. He exhibited exceptional diplomacy and professional skills with marked success, correlating the activities of his command with those of the air forces of the Far East. Through his impressive leadership, initiative and dedication to his duty, Colonel Cárdenas reflected very well on himself and his country, and his exemplary performance in service contributed to the success of the Allied air operations in the Southeastern Pacific."

Mexico did not receive any territory for its services in the war, but it did earn itself a place in the assembly of victorious countries that made up the United Nations and even a seat on the United Nations Security Council in 1946. It was also awarded several warplanes which modernized its archaic air force; the Bracero Program for legal temporary migration to the US for agricultural workers was renewed until 1964; and 39.3 million dollars in war compensations, a far more modest amount than that received by Brazil, the only other Iberoamerican country to dispatch troops. However, Mexico did not take advantage of the opportunity offered by the US to develop an air force with a significant presence in Latin America.

The legacy of the 201st Squadron

The Mexican Expeditionary Air Force was disolved in December 1945, and Mexico began to focus on other issues. The tributes, high praise and exaggerated official discourse ("You have the right to enjoy the title of heroes, bestowed upon you by your motherland") had been mostly diplomatic. When President Manuel Ávila Camacho left his post in 1946, any sense that the men would continue to be icons dissipated. The "gentleman president" returned to work on his ranch and died nine years later. To this day, he is the only Mexican president ever to send troops to fight overseas. The presidential sash was passed on to Miguel Alemán Velasco, the first civilian to ascend to the position following the Mexican Revolution. In the style of Mexican politics of the time, Alemán was careful not to pay tribute to the actions of soldiers nor to extol excessively the accomplishments of his predecessor. The new system sought to prevent the members of the 201st from becoming political figures with aspirations to public positions. It was Miguel Alemán who unveiled the monument to the FAEM in Chapultepec, but there was no heart in the gesture.

On June 8, 1946, a victory parade was held in London, the capital of the now dismembered British Empire, where a Mexican military contingent passed in front of King George VI and his family, Winston Churchill and other characters. Most of the allied countries marched, including Brazil, China, Transjordan and Mexico, but there were notable absences such as Poland and especially the USSR. Incredibly, the members of 201st Squadron were absent in the Victory Parade, with the exception of Justino Retana Reyes, who was the flag bearer. This inexplicable lack of memory was the beginning of a tendency to forget them.

The members of the Squadron did not stay close to each other physically, but they continued to be friends in spirit. In 1952, most of them received medals for bravery from the Filipino president, Elpidio Quirino. Many left the Mexican armed forces in order to pursue careers in commercial aviation or as instructors. Several formed the first wave of pilots of Aeroméxico, an airline founded in 1934 under the name *Aeronaves de México*. Its success and expertise meant that Mexicans began to view flying as a safe activity. One of the most prolific of these pilots was Ángel Sánchez Rebolledo, who went on to fly the presidential aircraft for four terms. Carlos Garduño was head pilot for the Bank of Mexico and later became the presidential pilot, along with Adolfo López Mateos. Radamés Gaxiola Andrade, the Squadron leader, was the deputy of the Presidential Guard and, later, the head of the PEMEX Department of Air Transport. He died when his aircraft crashed near Acapulco in 1966. The Squadron members who died in the Philippines and whose bodies could be recovered were buried in the mausoleum of Chapultepec.

IN MEMORY OF THE 201ST SQUADRON, IN A LITTLE-VISITED PART OF CHAPULTEPEC

Surprisingly, Mexican historians showed little interest in the Squadron: it became a subject more for television, radio and comic strips, often with historically inaccurate and unrealistic stories. Over in the States and other Allied countries, soldiers of the Second World War became the greatest generation; in Mexico they were soon all but forgotten. Sadly, in recent decades, the actions of the FAEM have been more well-known in the US, where many of them ultimately chose to live, than in their own homeland. There is only one survivor at the time of this writing: Carlos Garduño Núñez. When he dies, the extraordinary generation of which he was a part will have taken its last breath.

The 201st Squadron perfectly symbolizes the role that Mexico played in the Second World War: its involvement was not a deciding factor, but its conduct was impeccable. Mexico was the only country to protest against the annexation of Austria by Nazi Germany when the rest of the world turned a blind eye; it was the Mexicans agricultural workers who, in the words of the American geographer Don Mitchell, "saved the crops" in the US —America would not have been able to send so many men to the fighting front if there had not been a Mexican available to replace every farmer who went to fight. In addition, Mexico supplied the US with raw materials despite the risks involved, and its diplomatic capability and leadership succeeded in persuading almost all of the American hemisphere to declare war on the Axis. Nevertheless, Mexican politicians leaned more heavily on the feats of the FAEM. When the presidents and secretaries of the government went to Washington and spoke with poorly-disguised hypocrisy of "mutual sacrifice", they were doing everything possible to exaggerate the extent of their participation in the war, suggesting that Mexico's contribution to the defeat of the Axis was on a par with that of the US or even Brazil.

When the FAEM arrived in Nuevo Laredo, the representative of the Secretary of National Defense, Enrique A. Rojas, read out loud to the soldiers: "It is with great emotion that we attend the epilogue of this bloody war in which, faithful to its noble tradition, Mexico has raised its sword against imperialist anti-libertarians who would have exercised supremacy over the smoking ruins of vulnerable peoples." He then spoke about the "Indian of Guelatao" (Benito Juárez) and heavily criticized the "nations blinkered by the illusion of apocryphal greatness" who, unlike Mexico, had ignored the dangers of Nazism. Long gone were the days of the dalliances of Vasconcelos and Dr. Atl with Germany. This exaggerated speech was a calculated way of reminding people that barely six years earlier, the country had been on the verge of invasion by its "allies" (over oil expropiation) and that a new international order was due.

None of this, though, detracts from the honor and merit of the thirty pilots of the 201st Squadron, for whom the Second World War was very real: for those who went uncomplainingly to the fighting front to face hunger and danger, who fought in battles, who watched their comrades die. In the postwar world, its members were conveniently relegated and ignored by historians. There were tributes in the first decades, but as they started to pass away, the remaining pilots were even despised, to the point of not allowing them to parade at civic holidays. In the United States they received greater consideration from the academy.

Mexico's role in the war is acknowledged, in modest yet meaningful ways, in various places around the world. One such acknowledgement comes in the form of a plaque in Mexikoplatz, Vienna, thanking Mexico for being the only country to formally protest Hitler's erasure of Austria from the map. The inscription on the stone reads: "In March of 1938, Mexico was the only country to protest officially before the League of Nations the violent annexation of Austria by National Socialist Germany. In tribute to this act, the city of Vienna names this plaza after Mexico."

Another perhaps more heartfelt commemoration of Mexico's involvement is found, all but forgotten, in a monument on the outskirts of Manila. Despite its neglected state, it is still magnificent: an eagle devouring a serpent clutched in its outstretched claws. The monument was not, in fact, erected by the Philippine government, but by the members of the 201st Squadron themselves, in honor of those who would never return to their families —and some never even had a proper burial to find eternal rest. The monolith was designed by Miguel Moreno Arreola, the orphan who had joined the squadron and who carried the Mexican flag on the day of the welcome parade. Under the majestic, weathered eagle, a simple plaque pays tribute to the pilots' heroism:

The members of the
Mexican Expeditionary Air Force,
the 201st Fighter Squadron,
dedicate this monument to their brothers
who fell in the line of duty:

Cap. P. Rivas Martínez
Lt. J. Espinoza Fuentes
Lt. H. Espinoza Galván
2nd Lt. M. López Portillo
2nd Lt. F. Vega Santander

Glory to them.

MONUMENT IN MANILA, PHILIPPINES, ERECTED BY THE
MEMBERS OF THE 201ST SQUADRON BEFORE LEAVING
FOR MEXICO.

"ONE OF THE MEMBERS TOOK TWO STEPS FORWARD, SALUTED AND SAID IN AN UNWAVERING VOICE: *MISTER PRESIDENT, MY NAME IS CORPORAL ÁNGEL BOCANEGRA DEL CASTILLO. SIR, I WOULD LIKE TO REQUEST THAT A SCHOOL BE BUILT IN MY TOWN OF TEPOZTLÁN, MORELOS*".

APPENDIX I. THE 201ST SQUADRON

SQUADRON COMMANDER:
RADAMÉS GAXIOLA ANDRADE

SECOND IN COMMAND:
PABLO L. RIVAS MARTÍNEZ

WING "A"
ROBERTO LEGORRETA SICILIA
FERNANDO HERNÁNDEZ VEGA
CARLOS VARELA LANDINI
GRACO RAMÍREZ GARRIDO
JOSÉ LUIS PRATT RAMOS
MIGUEL URIARTE AGUILAR
DAVID CERÓN BEDOLLA

WING "B"
CARLOS GARDUÑO NÚÑEZ
JULIO CAL Y MAYOR SAUZ
REYNALDO PÉREZ GALLARDO
MIGUEL MORENO ARREOLA
PRAXEDIS LÓPEZ RAMOS
ÁNGEL SÁNCHEZ REBOLLO
FAUSTO VEGA SANTANDER

WING "C"
HÉCTOR ESPINOZA GALVÁN
JOAQUÍN RAMÍREZ VILCHIS
CARLOS RODRÍGUEZ CORONA
AMADOR SÁMANO PIÑA
RAÚL GARCÍA MERCADO
GUILLERMO GARCÍA RAMOS

MANUEL FARÍAS RODRÍGUEZ
JOSÉ ESPINOZA FUENTES

WING "D"
AMADEO CASTRO ALMANZA
JACOBO ESTRADA LUNA
JOSÉ LUIS BARBOSA CERDA
MARIO LÓPEZ PORTILLO
ROBERTO URIAS AVELEYRA
JAIME ZENIZO ROJAS
JUSTINO REYES RETINA

THE 30 PILOTS OF THE 201ST

APPENDIX II. ALL THE MEMBERS OF THE MEXICAN EXPEDITIONARY AIR FORCE (FAEM)

Below, a well-deserved tribute to the other Mexicans who contributed from the ground to the success of the 201st Squadron; a list which had never been published in its entirety. The following names are those who boarded the *Fairisle* for the Philippines.

Colonel
Antonio Cárdenas Rodríguez

Mayor

Enrique Sandoval Castarrica · Ricardo Blanco Cancino · Guillermo Linage Olguín

Captain 1°

Roberto Salido Beltrán · Radamés Gaxiola Andrade

Captain 2°

Jesús Blanco Ledezma · Jesús Carranza Hernández · Roberto Legorreta Sicilia · Samuel R. Pacheco Marín · Pablo Rivas Martínez

Lieutenant

Luis Álvarez Maytorena · Antonio Villar Gutiérrez · José Luis Barbosa Cerda · Julio Cal y Mayor Sauz · Amadeo Castro Almanza · José A. Cruz Abundis Cano · Héctor Espinosa Galván · José Espinosa Fuentes · Jacobo Estrada Luna · Carlos Garduño Núñez · Fernando Hernández Vega · Reynaldo Pérez Gallardo · Graco Ramírez Garrido · Joaquín Ramírez Vilchis · Armando

Rodríguez Contreras · Carlos Rodríguez Corona · Raúl Rodríguez Carreón · Ignacio Salinas Ramos · Amador Sámano Piña · Jesús Tapia Estrada · Carlos Varela Landini · César Velasco Cerón

Second Lieutenant

Guillermo Albert Robles · Ramón Caracas Enríquez · Jaime Cenizo Rojas · David Cerón Bedolla · Samuel Cueto Ramírez · Manuel Farías Rodríguez · Guillermo García Ramos · Raúl García Mercado · Luis Hurtado Tinajero · Mario López Portillo · Praxedis López Ramos · Miguel Moreno Arreola · José Luis Pratt Ramos · Justino Reyes Retana · Esteban Rubio Pérez · Ángel Sánchez Rebollo · José Miguel Uriarte Aguilar · Roberto Urías Abelleyra · Fausto Vega Santander

1st Sergeant

Rosendo Alarcón Santana · Eusebio Álvarez Huerta · Federico Arreola Romero · Enrique Barragán Aguilar · Aurelio Becerra Suárez · Carlos Beltrán Gutiérrez · Leonardo Beltrán Gutierrez · José Carlos Blanco Talavera · Alfonso Carbajal Aransolo · Teodoro Carrillo García · Miguel Castillo Torres · Francisco de la Vega Guzmán · Juvenal Delgado Meza · Manuel Espinosa González · Carlos Gálvez Pérez · César González Mata · Luis González Sánchez · Neftalí González Corona · Armando Grajeda Gómez · José Gutiérrez Gallegos · Jesús Herrera Zayas · Jesús Jurado Pulido · Felipe Manterila Cruz · Luis Martínez Miranda · Miguel Martínez Miranda · Miguel Martínez Márquez · Pedro Martínez de la Concha · Manuel Miranda Maillar · León Mondragón Hoyos · Luis Mondragón Hoyos · Carlos Obregón Martínez · Gregorio Ramírez Lowre · Daniel Ramos Méndez · Gonzalo Retana Guevara · Onésimo Spíndola Miranda · Agustín Velasco Alegría · Fernando Vergara García · Roberto Welsh Guerrero · Felipe Yépez Martínez

2nd Sergeant

Rafael Acuña Aguilar · José Álvarez Morales · Raúl Álvarez Ortega · Enrique Arenas Noreña · Jesús Arrona Calderón · Emereo Ávila Avilez · Leandro Ávila Sánchez · Francisco Bautista González · Juan Bautista Yáñez Camarena · Jacobo Bocanegra Velázquez · Alfredo Boybin Sánchez · Alberto Camacho García · Heriberto Cañete López · Sergio Carrillo Díaz · Horacio Castilleja Albarrán · Rubén Celis Piña · Héctor Cepeda Vázquez · Manuel Cervantes Ramos · Carlos Colín Portillo · Alfonso Cuéllar Ponce de León · Alfredo Chávez Hidalgo · Miguel Ángel Chávez Delgado · Gilberto de la Rosa Álvarez · Enrique Domínguez Rendón · Eduardo Eguiluz Rojas · Aristeo Elías Flores · Gilberto Escalante Arias · Julio Espíndola Miranda · Francisco Esquivel Reyes · Manuel Estrada Sosa · José Antonio Galindo Alfonseca · Luis Gallegos Mendoza · Raúl Gamas Quevedo · Humberto Gamboa Montoya · Ángel García Martínez · Jorge García Herrera · Luis García Vázquez · Ramón García Vega · Héctor G. Gómez Oaxaca · Ignacio Gómez Estrada · José León Gómez Domínguez · Andrés González Herrera · Fortino González Gudiño · Juan Antonio González Baez · Carlos Graillet Colorado · Daniel Grajeda Gómez · Pedro Guerra García · Jesús Guerrero Uribe · Jesús Gutiérrez Figueroa · Maximiliano Gutiérrez Marín · Luis Guzmán Rebeles · Óscar Hermosillo Ficachi · Ernesto Hernández May · José María Hernández Bailon · Adolfo Ireta Martínez · Genaro Jacinto Orduña · Fernando Juárez Jiménez · Dionisio Ledezma Espinosa · Rubén Ledezma Yañez · Andrés López Olivares · David Lozano Hernández · Abel Martínez Hernández · Agustín F. Martínez Cortés · Eduardo Moreno Brillas · Adolfo Ortiz Jiménez · Carlos Ortiz Moreno · Enrique C. Ortiz Jiménez · Moisés Osorio Domínguez · Armando Padilla Uribe · Eduardo Peredo Muñoz · Eugenio Pérez Fernández · Ismael Pérez Becerra · Luis Pérez Lara · José Ponce Olmos · Carlos Quintana Moreno · Pedro Ramírez Corona · José Rayón Varela · Alfonso Real Martínez · Guillermo Reyna Sánchez · Francisco Rodríguez Castañeda · Genaro Romero Parra

· José Luis Rubio del Riego · Mario Salcedo Cruces · Rogelio Salcedo Saldaña · José Sánchez García · Joaquín Sánchez Montes · Silvestre San Vicente Ovando · Francisco Sierra Ochoa · Jesús Silva Ruelas · Joaquín J. Silva Zamora · José de Jesús Solís Tapia · Julio Sorzano López · Leonardo Soto Rodríguez · Luis Soto Servín · Salvador Soto Uribe · Gustavo Toledo Belmont · José Torres Vara · José Luis Trejo Patiño · José Uriza López · Carlos Valdés León · Agustín Vallejo Montiel · Bernardo Vara Rangel · Filemón Vargas Morales · Salvador Vázquez Morales

Corporal

Raymundo Acosta Ordaz · Manuel Alcántar Torres · Luis Jorge Alfonso López · Alberto Almeida Sigueiros · Rodolfo Ambriz Martínez · Javier Armenta Sánchez · Lázaro Arrieta Saldaña · José Arroyo García · Eligio Barajas Espinosa · Ramiro Bastarrachea Gamboa · Justo Becerril Sosa · Angel Bocanegro del Castillo · Arnulfo Bonilla García · José Bonilla Domínguez · Fidel Borunda Salcedo · Gilberto Correa Juárez · Antonio Cruz Morales · Juan de Asco Beotegui · Francisco Elías Díaz Aguayo · Francisco Díaz Meraz · Gerardo Díaz Bolaños · Antonio Escalante Flores · Jorge Estrada Ochoa · Ignacio Fragoso Cedillo · Carlos Garay García · Alfredo García Orocio · Guillermo García González · Samuel Garrido Mendoza · Felipe González Labastida · Olegario Gómez Rodríguez · Manuel Guerrero Muñoz · Othón Gutiérrez Medina · Mario Luis Higuera Rábago · Javier Ibáñez Carrillo · Luis Jiménez Sánchez · Luis Mandujano Gallegos · Ernesto Martínez Trujillo · Pedro Martínez Pérez · Wenceslao Martínez Vázquez · David Mata Ramos · Alfredo Mendoza Mendoza · Bernandino Mendoza Hernández · Carlos Mendoza Jáuregui · Erasmo Meza Rivera · Fernando Miranda Gómez · Enrique Molina Pérez · Higinio Monroy Alvarado · Lino Morales Guadarrama · Sergio Morales Bernal · Manuel Munguía Moreno · José Muñoz Alvear · Luis Jorge Oviedo Villa · Ramiro Pérez Calvillo · Ricardo Quintal Pinzón · Armando Ramírez Campillo · Agustín Miguel Reséndez Mireles · Juan Reynoso Fuentes ·

Manuel Rico Badillo · Jesús Rivera Arce · Jaime Romano Reséndiz · Jesús Salas Olivas · Eduardo Sánchez Ortiz · David Santana García · Hugo Seaman Jiménez · Jorge Serralde Ganot · Héctor Tello Pineda · Ricardo Tinoco Lima · Gilberto Tovar García · Rafael Valdés Balleza · Raúl Vargas Gómez · Rasendil Várguez Magaña · Alfredo Vega Fernández

Soldier

Carlos Centeno Medina · Rafael Burguete Pascasio · Esteban Carballo Reyes · Gustavo Díaz Campomanes · Raúl Esteva Aquino · Antonio Enríquez Guerrero · Bernardo Gómez de los Santos · Diego López Félix · Juan López Murillo · Enrique Moedano Gómez · Fernando Nava Musa · Leoncio Pérez Juárez · Francisco Ramos Méndez · Herminio Sanchez Luis · José Sánchez García Nuño · José de Jesús Segura Ríos · Rubén Silva Richards · Felipe Soto Martínez · Alfonso Vega Gómez · Arnulfo Vieyra Pozos · Juan Villafaña Ávila · Mario Zamora Aguilar

BIBLIOGRAPHY

Aviation History (2006), *World War II: Mexican Air Force Helped Liberate the Philippines*. Aviation History Magazine, December 2006.

Beezley, William H. *et al*, (2017). *Problems in Modern Mexican History: Sources and Interpretations*. USA: Rowman & Littlefield Publishers

Bennighof, Michael, (2015) *Great Pacific War: Mexico at war*. Avalanche Press.

Cedillo, Juan A, (2007). *Los nazis en México*. México: Debate.

García, Jerry, (2014). *Looking Like the Enemy: Japanese Mexicans, the Mexican State, and US Hegemony, 1897–1945*. USA: University of Arizona Press.

Greer, Thomas H. (1983). "Other Training Programs," in *The Army Air Forces in World War II*, Volumen 6 de "Men and Planes", Washington: Office of Air Force History.

Haro, Dany (Producer), & Mancilla, Víctor (Director). (2006). The Forgotten Eagles [Película]. USA: 201 Productions.

Hooper, Andy (2011). "Las Aguilas Aztecas". *The Drink Tank*, No. 300, pp. 58-65.

Jerade Dana, Miriam (2015). Antisemitismo en Vasconcelos: antiamericanismo, nacionalismo y misticismo estético, en *Mexican Studies/Estudios Mexicanos*, Vol. 31, Issue 2, Summer 2015, pág. 248–286. University of California.

Jones, Halbert (2014). *The War Has Brought Peace to Mexico: World War II and the Consolidation of the Post-Revolutionary State*. University of New Mexico   Press.

Kenney, George, (1987). *General Kenney Reports: A Personal History of the Pacific War*. Office of Air Force History, USAF

Leonard, Thomas M. *et al,* (2006). Latin America During World War II. USA: Rowman & Littlefield Publishers.

Marshall, George C. Foundation & Virginia Military Institute, (2002). *The Journal of Military History.* Volume 66, Issues 3-4.

Mitchell, Don, (2012). *They saved the crops: Labor, Landscape, and the Struggle over Industrial Farming in Bracero-Era California.* USA: University of Georgia Press.

Paz, Ma. Emilia, (1997). *Strategy, Security, and Spies: Mexico and the U.S. as Allies in World War II.* USA: Penn State University Press.

Sandoval Castarrica, Enrique, (1946). *Historia Oficial de la Fuerza Aérea Expedicionaria Mexicana.* Secretaría de la Defensa Nacional.

Schwab, Stephen I, (2002). "The Role of the Mexican Expeditionary Air Force in World War II: Late, Limited, but Symbolically Significant." The Journal of Military History, vol. 66, no. 4, pp. 1115–1140.

Vázquez Lozano, Gustavo (2006). *El siglo XX en la mirada de Antonio Arias Bernal.* Mexico: Instituto Cultural de Aguascalientes.

Vega Rivera, José G., (1997). *The Mexican Expeditionary Air Force in World War II: The Organization, Training, and Operations of the 201st Squadron.* Tesis presentada al Air Command and Staff College, Alabama, USA.

ABOUT THE AUTHOR

Gustavo Vázquez Lozano was born in Mexico. He has authored over thirty titles in English and Spanish, and collaborates with several printed media in Mexico and the United States. A graduate of Liberal Studies in NYU, and Creative Writing in Wesleyan University, he has written extensively about early Christianity, and Mexico´s history. He is also a successful fiction author with award-winning novels.

El elefante que sonreía (The elephant that smiled), a thriller, tells the story of a Mexican-American circus in Veracruz during the Depression era, and the strange cult that develops around the tomb of a girl who was murdered. *La Estrella del Sur* (The Southern Star) is a sea novel about a boy who is abducted by modern-day pirates.

Among his most recent publications are *60 años de soledad*, the life of Empress Carlota after the failed Mexican Empire (Random House, 2019), and a new novel, *Xico* (Libros de México, 2020), both met with critical success. He lives in Aguascalientes, Mexico.

The publisher Libros de México, founded in 2011, produces general interest content for Spanish- and English-speaking readers on topics including history, science, social studies, and literary and artistic content. To view our catalogue and recieve updates, news and offers, visit https://www.facebook.com/librosdemexico
www.librosdemexico.org

www.ingramcontent.com/pod-product-compliance
Lightning Source LLC
LaVergne TN
LVHW091157080426
835509LV00006B/727